PRIMARY
FOUNDATIONS

PSHE and citizenship

AGES 9-11

Duncan Smith

CONTENTS

Author
Duncan Smith

Editorial
Dulcie Booth

Series designer
Lynne Joesbury

Designer
Paul Cheshire

Illustrations
Annabel Spencely

Cover photograph
Digital Vision

ACKNOWLEDGEMENTS
The Publishers would like to thank: **British Institute of Traffic Education Research** for the use of statistics on page 119 which appeared in 'Road safety education for children transferring from primary to secondary school' by C V Platt et al © July 2000, BITER (2000, Department of Environment Transport and the Regions). **Conoco and Du Pont** for the use of information on pages 138-140 and page 151 which were first used in the Conoco Services to Education Resource Pack *Understanding our Environment* © 1996, Crystal Presentations Ltd (1996, Conoco Services to Education). **The Equal Opportunities Commission** for the use of statistics in items 3 and 4 on page 157 which appeared in a press release 20th December 1999 entitled *Women and Men at the Millennium - EOC Reviews of the Century* © 1999, The Equal Opportunities Commission (1999, The EOC). www.eoc.org.uk. **Her Majesty's Stationery Office** for the use of statistics on page 157 items 1, 2 and 5 from *Labour Market Statistics ONS 1999, Average Hourly Earnings ONS New Earnings Survey 1999* and the DfEE website www.dfee.gov.uk for Types of Jobs. © 1999, Crown copyright (1999, Her Majesty's Stationery Office). Crown copyright is produced with the permission of the Controller of Her Majesty's Stationery Office. **Living Earth** for the use of statistics on page 152-53 from 'Cameroon Environmental Education Project' www.livingearth.org.uk.

**Published by
Scholastic Ltd,**
Villiers House,
Clarendon Avenue,
Leamington Spa,
Warwickshire
CV32 5PR
**Printed by Bell &
Bain Ltd, Glasgow**
Text © Duncan
Smith © 2001
Scholastic Ltd
Visit our website at
www.scholastic.co.uk

2 3 4 5 6 7 8 9 0
2 3 4 5 6 7 8 9 0

British Library Cataloguing-in-Publication Data
A catalogue record for this book is available from
the British Library.

ISBN 0-439-01859-5

Introduction

This book suggests how PSHE and citizenship can be divided into manageable teaching units for nine- to eleven-year-olds. Each themed chapter provides two units of work. These units are often complementary to each other and therefore you should choose one or other as appropriate to your needs. Most of the units can be used to form the basis of a substantial chunk of personal, social and health education work – perhaps over a half term – and by providing progressive lesson plans show how PSHE and citizenship can be sequenced. The grids at the beginning of each unit are intended to aid medium-term planning. They highlight (in bold) the enquiry questions covered by the lesson plans as well as additional enquiry questions which could be used to extend the unit further. The grids can also be used to help plan links that PSHE and citizenship has with other subjects across the curriculum, especially literacy and numeracy. (ICT links are given within the lesson plans themselves.) By providing a broad overview, the grids also help with planning the resources that you will need to collect in preparation for the unit.

The introductions to each unit provide some background information that you may find useful when working with the lesson plans. There is also guidance provided on matching learning opportunities to a range of ability levels.

Renewing an old debate

There has long been a debate about the precise nature and contribution of PSHE and citizenship to the curriculum. Within schools you would be unlikely to find disagreement over the basic need for the curriculum to promote the spiritual, moral, cultural, mental and physical development of children as well as preparing them for the opportunities, responsibilities and experiences of adult life. Indeed, schools are required to include these areas in their curriculum. Neither, one suspects, would there be much disagreement over the essential ingredients of that programme. Instead, much of the debate has been focused on issues of where to fit the provision within the existing curriculum structure and, equally importantly, what teaching methods and approaches to employ. Increasing pressures and demands from other areas of the curriculum have meant that difficult decisions about priorities have had to be made. The non-statutory guidance in the National Curriculum (2000) goes some way in answering some of these questions by providing a model which demonstrates progression, continuity and breadth of opportunity. This book has taken these guidelines as its basis and shown how manageable units of work can result from them.

Why is PSHE and citizenship important?

There are a number of good reasons that support the inclusion of personal, social and health education and citizenship in the school curriculum. The first is that children are entitled to an education which includes a personal and social dimension in much the same way as they have an entitlement to the provision of literacy and numeracy. Such a provision recognises the need for children to understand and appreciate fully the basis of human and interpersonal behaviour and how this affects the individual, the group and the community as a whole. This will enable children to have the confidence and independence that will help them to become informed and responsible citizens.

A second fundamental part of this provision is that it contributes to the development of children's social and interpersonal skills. These skills will enable them to interrelate effectively with their peer group, with parents and teachers, and with other adults. They will also be made more aware of their own worth as individuals.

The final benefit that this entitlement offers is the opportunity to hold an open and honest exploration of individual and community attitudes, values and beliefs within a safe and supportive environment. This will help children to assess their responsibilities and rights as members of a community and to appreciate diversity and differences between individuals.

To sum up, PSHE and citizenship is important because it helps children to develop mutual respect and support for each other; it encourages them to make informed decisions about issues discussed;

it supports the learning skills of life, such as:
- awareness of and care for others and the environment
- learning to state effectively one's own feelings
- being constructively critical and questioning
- being responsible for one's own behaviour and learning.

PSHE and citizenship in school and the community

In school, a part of the 'community', there is a need for the understanding of the importance of good social and interpersonal skills. These are the essential building blocks for creating a supportive learning environment. Effective and meaningful relationships between the children themselves and between the children and the staff lie at the heart of an 'achieving' school.

Parents and carers are also a part of that community, and the development of children's social and interpersonal skills is perceived by many parents to be a key responsibility of the school. At the same time, many people would regard this as a goal only achievable through a genuine partnership between home and school.

The community in its wider context of the society in which we live frequently expresses its shock and outrage at some of the extreme antisocial behaviour of certain individuals and groups. There is often a sense that society is entitled to better standards of behaviour, but this is often accompanied by a lack of understanding of how this might be achieved.

PSHE and citizenship for nine- to eleven-year-olds

In this book the themes reflect the areas that have been highlighted in the National Curriculum non-statutory guidelines on PSHE and citizenship. These provide an appropriate context to explore social and interpersonal issues, including health, environment and relationships. Each unit begins by establishing what the children already know and understand about the topics. They are encouraged to build up their knowledge through various experiences and exchanges with their peer group, family and friends. A range of approaches are used to promote understanding, including stories, role-play and art, and suggestions for discussion and debate are provided.

Each unit identifies general and specific skills related to the theme and begins by allowing the children to 'audit' their own skills as a basis for building further competencies. All activities have a skill-building component, and also allow for the exploration and examination of personal values and beliefs. Within the themes, children can explore their own personal expectations as they relate to some of these important issues. They will also be given opportunities to consider the expectations of others, whether they be friends, family or the wider community.

Building healthy relationships

CHAPTER 1

This chapter identifies and examines two increasingly important areas of children's personal and social development at this stage in their lives.

The first is an understanding of the increasing importance of teamwork in both work and play, whether in school or leisure activities, or a more general ability to work collaboratively with different groups of people on a specific task.

The second key area of children's social development featured in this chapter is their growing perception of a wider community beyond their own town or country.

Building a team

It is important for children to understand that there are principles associated with good teamwork. They should learn to apply these principles in familiar and less familiar contexts.

Working in a team requires a spirit of collaboration and compromise as well as a shared purpose and a sense of joint responsibility. But the children should also appreciate that successful teams need diversity, in terms of the knowledge, skills and values that their different members may possess. Teams, although they need to be united, should also be able to cope with individualism and the children need to realise that there can be strength in diversity, as well as dangers. Understanding and managing conflict are two important prerequisites of successful teamwork.

Children at this age should begin to identify and assess their own competencies for working in a team and appreciate how these can complement other people's strengths. At the same time, they need to be able to recognise their own weak areas as far as teamwork is concerned. Trying to do something about these weaknesses is another vital part of the learning process. The children need to appreciate that individual weaknesses in team members require the support of everyone if that team is to succeed.

Building a nation

Many children of this age will have travelled to other countries, though probably only as tourists. They will have encountered views and opinions about nationality and race, and the associated issues of discrimination, prejudice and bias, possibly from their own community and certainly from the media.

Issues of citizenship and how individuals perceive their own nationality and identity clearly relate to how individuals see themselves, and relate particularly to their own level of self-esteem, confidence and self-awareness. Equally, these perceptions have a bearing on how people view others who are of a different nationality or class.

Learning contexts

The chapter introduces these key perspectives progressively, first from the point of view of the individual child and the familiar classroom or home setting, then moving on to explore them in the context of the wider community and country.

The identification and examination of personal feelings, as with any topic related to the personal and social development of the child, are important elements in the learning process. Emphasis is placed on drawing out this aspect of the learning throughout the chapter in order for the children to gain confidence in their ability to express their feelings in a safe and supportive environment.

Building a team

This unit focuses on helping children to understand the importance and significance of teamwork in their own lives.

At a number of levels, and in a number of contexts, children are increasingly expected to be able to work together effectively in groups. In order to do this successfully they need to understand the processes involved and develop and demonstrate both the skills and qualities required. Failure to create the potential for a good team in the first instance, and then maintain it as a coherent unit, can lead to frustration and disappointment and, equally importantly, an unwillingness to work in that manner again.

Children, like adults, when given a group task, become preoccupied with the task, starting it, seeing it progress and completing it. Considerations for the people in the team are of secondary importance and are often totally neglected. Consequently, the task may be completed, and completed well, but at a cost to the coherence of the whole team or individuals within it. This unit addresses these considerations.

The first activity identifies some of the goals of a team and shows how important it is for those goals to be shared by all its individual members. The second focuses on some of the important ingredients of successful teamwork, understanding responsibilities, defining strengths and weaknesses and matching skills to strengths.

Later activities deal with the importance of leadership in a team, stressing the importance of the leader's responsibility for the task, the people and the processes. Another indicates that all teams, even the successful ones, encounter problems – often conflicts of interest, personalities, priorities or standards and shows how successful teams learn to identify problems early and quickly, and deal with them.

The activities in this unit allow the children to practise and reflect on the two key aspects of teamwork, the task and the process. They give them opportunities to assess their skills and success at achieving an appropriate outcome, not only in terms of the task, but also in how they achieved it. They should not only be able to assess the quality of the task but should also be able to identify the ways in which the team has 'grown' and 'matured' in the process.

Unit: Building a team

Enquiry questions	Learning objectives	Teaching activities	Further teaching activities	Learning outcomes	Cross-curricular links
What is a team? What characteristics do teams have in common?	● Learn that there are different types of teams. ● Understand that teams have shared goals with which everyone in the team must agree.	Discuss what makes a team and consider shared goals. Work in small teams on plans for a local leisure centre.	● Draw up a successful team for a particular project using the names of famous people or people they know. ● Research successful teams from the past from sport, science, technology or exploration. ● Write a speech to give to a team of people just about to undertake a dangerous expedition. What would you say to them?	*Children:* ● apply understanding of shared goals to a familiar experience of team membership ● apply understanding of shared goals to a less familiar context ● display positive attitudes towards the processes of agreeing and sharing goals	English: speaking and listening.
How do teams deal with difficult individuals? What can teams gain from individuals?	● Understand that teams need people to be themselves. ● Appreciate that individuals need to recognise their strengths and weaknesses for the sake of the team.	Draw up a profile of an imaginary individual, listing strengths and weaknesses. Discuss ways of identifying and improving weaknesses.	● Draw up a 'rogues' gallery of 'difficult' individuals who have been members of teams. ● Role-play a difficult situation between a teacher and someone who thinks they 'know better' and should be in charge. ● Design a team of 'famous' individuals for a particular task and write a story about what happened.	● appreciate both the advantages and disadvantages of the 'individual' within the team ● appreciate that the whole team has some responsibility for helping 'individuals' within it ● draw on their own experiences to contribute to the discussion	English: using adjectives to describe personality.
What makes a team successful? How can teams achieve successful collaboration?	● Appreciate that different kinds of knowledge and skills are required if a team is to be successful.	Identify and use the varied skills of members of a team. Design a contract for each member.	● Write a speech to give to a team which has failed to achieve its ambition to sail around the world. What would you say to them? ● Draw up a checklist for 'making a team work'. ● Design a contract for someone for a different project (using photocopiable page 108).	● understand the idea of combining knowledge and skills in a team to make it successful ● demonstrate appreciation of the variety of the inputs required ● assess an individual's knowledge or ability to do the job he or she is being asked to perform ● see the gaps in the groups' knowledge or skills and be able to identify ways of dealing with them	Geography: holiday destinations. English: writing contracts.
What makes a good leader? How can a team support its leader?	● Know that the leader of a team has to have certain knowledge, skills and qualities to be successful. ● Understand that good leaders have to look after the people in the team as well as manage the task.	Discuss the qualities that leaders need to have. List the skills, qualities and knowledge required by a good headteacher. Discuss this list with the headteacher.	● Design a job advertisement looking for someone to lead a group of children on an activity/adventure holiday. ● Produce an evaluation checklist for that leader so that he or she could self-assess his or her performance. ● Write a letter from someone who has led a team, and is leaving, to the person who is taking over, saying what they have learned.	● understand that all three areas (knowledge, skills and qualities) are important for good leadership ● identify a range of areas of knowledge, skills and qualities ● use their own experiences to draw up these lists ● question the headteacher about the importance of particular areas of knowledge, or specific skills and qualities	History: famous leaders. PE: famous sportspeople. English: speaking and listening.
What kinds of problems can teams encounter? What types of problem-solving strategies can teams use?	● Understand that some conflict within teams is inevitable ● Learn about different strategies to cope with, and resolve, conflict.	Discuss the causes of conflict and how these are expressed. Consider appropriate ways of resolving conflict.	● List a set of problems that might be encountered by a team of people walking from Land's End to John o'Groat's. ● Design a conflict resolution charter for teams. ● Design a board game which demonstrates how to deal with a particular problem of conflict in a group.	● distinguish between discussion, argument and conflict ● distinguish between actions and words as causes of conflict ● reason the possible solutions to conflict ● articulate the feelings and emotions brought on by such confrontations.	English: completing statements in response to pictures.

CHAPTER 1
BUILDING HEALTHY RELATIONSHIPS

Building a team

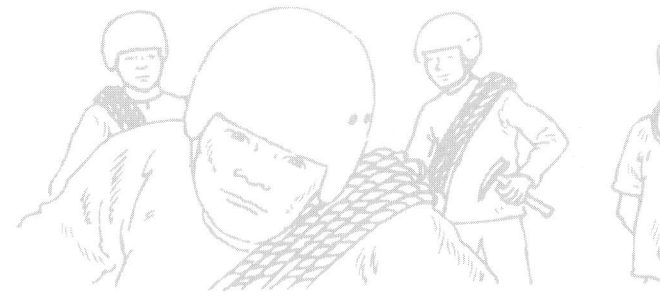

1 hour What is a team?

Learning objectives
● Learn that there are different types of teams.
● Understand that teams have shared goals with which everyone in the team must agree.

Lesson organisation
Introduction to focus the lesson and initial teacher-led discussion with visual stimulus; small-group activities and discussions; plenary.

What you need and preparation
Collect a range of photographs depicting different types of teams, such as a football, netball or hockey team, a motor racing team, or an orchestra. You will also need a board or flipchart. Make copies of photocopiable pages 103 and 104. Provide writing materials. You may also want to provide a large sheet of paper for publishing a class list of ideas on working as a team.

What to do
15 mins Introduction
Introduce the focus of the lesson, explaining that the word 'team' refers to a special group of people. Ask the children: *When I say the word 'team', give me another word that comes into your mind.* Allow them to make their own suggestions but help them with ideas such as: *rules, together, play, compete, support, friends, mates* or *help* if these are not given. List the words on the board as they come up. Ask the children to explain some of the words listed.

Use the photographs of different types of teams to introduce the following ideas about what 'team' can mean:
● The word 'team' can be used to describe a range of different groups, not just people who compete in sport. Invite the children to think of some examples of different types of teams, perhaps actors in a play, or employees working on a project in an office.
● Sometimes the word 'group' is used to describe a collection of people, rather than 'team'. Do the children think that 'groups' are different from 'teams' and, if so, why, and in what ways? Would they, for instance, regard people on a coach holiday as a team?

Allow the discussion to develop but point out that a 'team' of people has a set of shared goals or objectives and that this is what makes them different from a group. The members of a team also work together in an organised way to achieve these goals by agreeing aims and deadlines and what it is they have to do.

Ask the children to think of a team of which they are a member and list the shared goals that they think they have. Ask them if all the members of their team would agree with these goals.

Organise the children into small groups and ask each group to think of the shared goals two different types of teams might have. Either allocate teams for each group to discuss or allow the children to choose. Encourage them to choose diverse teams, for example a cricket team and a team of volunteers cleaning up a canal. Give two copies of photocopiable page 103 to each group and ask them to use the first part of these to record their thoughts on the goals for each team. Encourage the children to think beyond the basic notions of being successful, winning or beating the other team and to consider ideas such as loyalty, or being supportive of each other. Then ask the children to think about the goals that the team's supporters or the team's manager might expect of them. Tell them to use the second part of the photocopiable sheets to record their discussion.

Vocabulary
goals
objectives
collaboration
loyalty
achievement
sharing
participation
agreement

30 mins Development
Talk about a team of designers working together to select facilities for a new leisure centre (a swimming pool, sauna, games areas, changing rooms and so on). Don't give them too many ideas as their task is to come up with their own! Remind them of who will use the facilities.

Organise the children into small groups and give each group a copy of photocopiable page 104. Tell them that they are a team who design leisure centres and that their task is to brainstorm

ideas for the contents of a new leisure centre for their town. A final list of six major facilities must be agreed. Ask the children to record their initial ideas and their six chosen facilities on the photocopiable sheet.

15 mins **Plenary**
Discuss the brainstormed ideas. Ask:
● Did everyone get a chance to offer an idea?
● Was it easy to agree on a list of facilities?
● Did people listen to what was being said?
● Did anyone feel that their ideas were not listened to?
Discuss ways of improving the process of sharing and agreeing ideas. Publish these suggestions as a class record for use in later work.

Differentiation
Support the less able children in the first activity by allocating them teams to work with. Give them one or two examples of the goals these teams might have and ask them to think of others. Provide them with one or two visual stimuli for the leisure centre activity.

More able children could be encouraged to think of wider definitions and distinctions between groups and teams in the first activity, and give examples.

Assessing learning outcomes
Are the children able to apply their understanding of shared goals to a familiar experience of team membership? Are they able to apply their understanding of shared goals to a less familiar context? Do the children display positive attitudes towards the processes of agreeing and sharing goals? Are they able to apply their learning to the group activity?

1 hour How do teams deal with difficult individuals?

What you need and preparation
Prepare sets of cards with pictures of individuals made from photocopiable page 105, enough for one card for each pair. Make a copy of photocopiable page 106 for each pair and copies of photocopiable page 107 as required. Provide suitable writing materials to complete the sheets.

What to do
25 mins **Introduction**
Introduce the idea that, although a team of people has to work or play together and have a shared aim or goal, there are opportunities for individuals to display and use their unique talents. Suggest that, in some cases, talented individuals in teams who are not allowed to 'shine' may become very unhappy and discontented.

Ask the children to give examples from their own interests, perhaps football or music, where they know of teams in which there are 'special' individuals. Encourage them to define what makes that person 'special', yet still part of the team: *He is very skilful. She is very confident.*

Divide the children into pairs and give each pair one of the picture cards made from photocopiable page 105 and a copy of photocopiable page 106. Explain that their task is to draw up an imaginary profile of that individual using some of the ideas provided on the sheet and more of their own. These should be listed under the headings 'Strengths' and 'Weaknesses'.

Give the pairs ten minutes to do this exercise, then arrange two pairs into groups of four and ask them to compile a complete list of all the strengths and weaknesses they have thought of.

CHAPTER I
BUILDING HEALTHY RELATIONSHIPS

Building a team

Vocabulary
individual
strengths
personality
weaknesses
discontented
frustrated
emotions
jealousy
composure
confidence
self-assured
self-image

20 mins **Development**
Suggest that it is important for people to appreciate their own weaknesses as these may affect the smooth working of a team. They may, for example, have a habit of not listening, or of doing things without telling other people. Point out that the individual, and the other members of his or her team, need to work together to help sort out any weaknesses as this will be for everyone's benefit.

Ask each group to select one of the weaknesses identified in their list and write down three things the individual could do to improve and three different things other members of the team could do to help that individual.

15 mins **Plenary**
Discuss with the children what they see as the positive aspects of people with individualistic personalities – they may be very self-confident, self-assured, outspoken, and so on. Then ask about the kinds of feelings that this type of individual can create in others – jealousy, confidence, anger, composure. Point out that these are contrasting feelings.

Ask the children how they would respond to someone accusing them of being more concerned about themselves and their individual performance than with the success of the team. Discuss their thoughts on this.

Differentiation
Children are likely to identify more with the negative than the positive aspects and you may need to help them think of positive emotions and feelings.

More able children could develop the idea of individual creativity or use a thesaurus to find more challenging words to describe personality, such as 'impetuous'.

Assessing learning outcomes
Do the children appreciate both the advantages and disadvantages of the 'individual' within the team? Do they appreciate that the whole team has some responsibility for helping individuals within it? Are they able to draw on their own experiences to contribute to the discussions?

Follow-up activity
Children could complete the task on photocopiable page 107, 'I think… what do you think?'

1 hour What makes a team successful?

Learning objective
Appreciate that different kinds of knowledge and skills are required if a team is to be successful.

What you need and preparation
Gather together some pictures or drawings of a well-known holiday destination, possibly Spain, France or Florida. You will also need brochures and magazines with holiday information on your chosen destination. Make one copy of photocopiable page 108 for each child, plus a few extra, and provide writing materials.

What to do
30 mins **Introduction**
Introduce the idea that successful teams use all the knowledge and skills that they have available. Before they start to work together they find out about the skills and knowledge of each person in the team, related to the task. This then allows everyone to do something that they are good at, or enjoy. The best teams also work out where they need extra help – a mountaineering expedition might hire a local guide or a team designing a car might use the advice of an engineer.

Divide the class into groups of three and explain that each group has to prepare a 'Responsibility chart' for planning and organising a holiday. Suggest that the children should

include in their 'group' another 'extra' person they know, perhaps a parent, or an older brother or sister, who has the appropriate knowledge or skills to help with this planning exercise.

You may need to help the children get started by giving them some planning headings, such as travelling options, currency, language information, what to do, food and clothing, and so on. Explain to them that their task is to decide who they think is the best person in their group to take responsibility for planning those chosen areas, based on their knowledge, experience and skills. For example, someone who is good at maths could be responsible for working out the exchange rates. Use the pictures or drawings of the holiday destination as stimulus for this part of the activity.

Ask the children to make a note of any aspects of the holiday about which no one within the group has any knowledge or skills. Ask them: *Where do you think you might get help for this area?*

🕔15 mins Development

Each small group should then use a copy of photocopiable page 108 to design a 'contract' for each group member, including any 'extra' adult helpers. It should state:
● What knowledge or skills the person has, and in what particular areas.
● Why these areas are important to the success of the holiday.
● How long they have to prepare the information or complete the task.

All the individuals concerned should be consulted and agree with what is being asked of them. They should also have the opportunity to add any of their strengths that they think the group may have missed.

Ask each of the groups to begin by identifying the knowledge elements for each holiday and ask them: *Can you justify why this sort of information is important? How do you know your chosen person has this knowledge?*

At the next stage, ask each group to identify the skills they have identified as being required. Ask them: *Have you seen your chosen person demonstrate these skills?*

Finally, ask if they think the people they have chosen have any special qualities that will be valuable: *He is dependable, he wouldn't let us down.* Do they think that they have a good planning team?

🕔15 mins Plenary

Discuss how easy it was to assess people's knowledge and skills accurately. *Do you think you got it right?* Discuss differences of opinion in the assessment between what the group thought and what the individual thought and consider any additional 'strengths' identified by individuals that the group missed.

Differentiation
Less able children will require help to identify the different areas of expertise required. Encourage the more able children to identify more precise levels of skill, such as the ability to map-read or calculate travel times. More able children could also be challenged to work on a particular problem that could occur on a holiday: *If someone is taken ill, who would deal with this?*

Assessing learning outcomes
Do the children understand the idea of combining knowledge and skills in a team to make it successful? Does their work on the expertise required demonstrate their appreciation of the variety of the inputs required? Are the children able to assess an individual's knowledge or ability to do the job he or she is being asked to perform? Can the children see the gaps in the group's knowledge or skills and are they able to identify ways of dealing with them?

Lesson organisation
Initial teacher-led introduction; group activity and discussion; plenary.

Vocabulary
knowledge
skill
qualities
ability
personality
competent
reliability
collaboration
compromise
honesty
value
worth

ICT opportunities
● Produce and print off the 'contract' for each member of the team on the computer.
● Children could e-mail the 'extra' person in the group during the planning exercise.

Follow-up activity
Consider any additional help or information that might be needed, such as using a camcorder to record the holiday or finding out about special places or events in that country. Groups should identify all possible sources of this additional information, including the Internet.

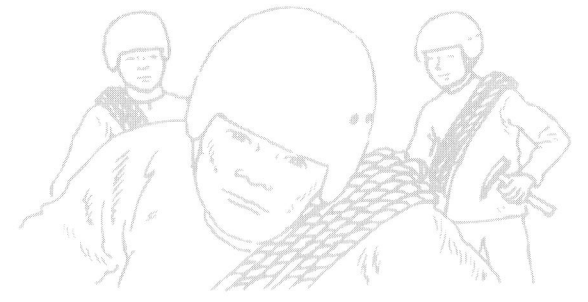

CHAPTER I
BUILDING HEALTHY RELATIONSHIPS

Building a team

① What makes a good leader?
hour

What you need and preparation
A collection of photographs or drawings of leaders – these could be quite famous people, such as sportspeople, politicians or military figures, or simply leaders of school teams. Be careful to include a good gender, as well as ethnic, mix of pictures. Supply writing materials, including large sheets of paper for lists. Make copies of photocopiable page 109 (for follow-up activity).

What to do
25 **Introduction**
mins Tell the children that a successful leader is someone with a certain amount of knowledge about the task to be completed, certain skills to enable them to complete the task and certain qualities to help them lead the team they are working with.

Ask them to think about the qualities needed to be the team captains for the school's netball or football teams. The team captain is likely to be one of the best players, he or she will probably have motivational skills and may also be an exemplary figure. Ask:
● what knowledge the team captain should have
● what skills the team captain should possess
● and what qualities he/she should have as a person.

Use the photographs of the various leaders you have collected to discuss the skills of other leaders.

Develop the idea by inviting the children to propose some humorous suggestions of leaders for the following (they could use famous people or people known to them, but try to prevent it getting too personal!):
● to lead a team of people on a mountaineering expedition
● to lead a team of people on a 'Round the World' yacht race
● to lead a team of people on a safari
● to lead a football team
● to conduct an orchestra.

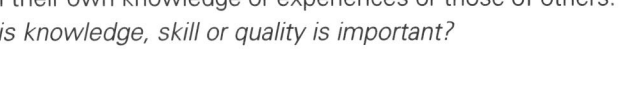

20 **Development**
mins Divide the class into three groups. Tell them to imagine that the headteacher is about to retire and that they have been given the job of appointing a replacement. Explain that each group is going to identify the three main areas that are required in order to be a good leader:
● what knowledge the headteacher should have
● what skills this person should possess
● and what qualities he/she should have as a person.

Each group could take on all three aspects of the task, or give different members of the group responsibility for deciding on knowledge, skills and qualities. Suggest to the groups that they should try to rank their ideas for each category in order. Supply each group with a large piece of paper to list these ideas on.

At the end of the task, display the lists from the three groups and ask the class to vote for their top three or four priorities in each of the three categories. Suggest that they base their choices for these three categories on their own knowledge or experiences or those of others. Ask them: *How do you know that this knowledge, skill or quality is important?*

Learning objectives
● Know that the leader of a team has to have certain knowledge, skills and qualities to be successful.
● Understand that good leaders have to look after the people in the team as well as manage the task.

Lesson organisation
Initial teacher-led introduction and stimulus activity; teacher-led discussion with the whole class; group activity and whole-class discussion; plenary.

Vocabulary
leadership
management
decisions
successful
experience
responsibility
delegation
determination
goals
achievement

ICT opportunities
● The letter to the headteacher could be word-processed.
● Use the Internet to carry out research on famous leaders.

15 mins **Plenary**

Invite the headteacher to come into the class and go through the children's list of ideas and comment on them from his or her own experience. Encourage the headteacher to add any areas of knowledge, skills or qualities that he or she feels have been forgotten.

At the end of the session, remind the children of the three categories of 'expertise' required of a good leader: knowledge, skills and qualities. Ask the children to nominate famous people they know about who they think would make good leaders.

Differentiation

Give less able children a key phrase, such as: 'A good leader has to be able to…' or 'A good leader has to know about…' to help them understand the three different categories.

Less able children are likely to display a narrow focus when choosing a new headteacher, while others will have a wider perspective. Provide different key words on cards to stimulate the less able and encourage the more able to think about the headteacher's responsibilities outside the school.

Assessing learning outcomes

Do the children understand that all three areas (knowledge, skills and qualities) are important for good leadership? Can they identify a range of areas of knowledge, skills and qualities? Are the children able to use their own experiences to draw up lists? Can they question the headteacher about the importance of particular areas of knowledge, or specific skills and qualities?

Follow-up activities
● Use photocopiable page 109, 'My leadership ambition', to detail what kind of team, activity, or past event each individual would like to lead, and the reasons for their choice.
● Ask the children to work in groups of six to create a page for the school newspaper. Tell each group to appoint a leader to allocate tasks and organise the page. After the task, discuss how well each leader carried out his or her responsibilities.

1 hour What kind of problems can teams encounter?

What you need and preparation

Prepare two charts for the initial stimulus activity. The first chart should have the heading 'Things that happen to me' and have two key statements on it:
● I get angry with someone when they say…
● I get angry with someone when they do…

Prepare a second chart with the same statements as above but with the heading: 'Things that I see happening to others…'

You will also need a board or flipchart, a copy of photocopiable page 110 for each group and writing materials.

What to do

25 mins **Introduction**

Ask the children if they think that conflict and disagreement are caused mainly by what people do (or don't do) to each other or what they say (or don't say) to each other, or both. Ask them for a few examples from their own experience: *What have people done (or said) to you to make you angry or cause you to stop being friends?* Then ask them to think of an example for the second category – things not done or said.

Distinguish for the children between actions or words that cause casual or short-term disagreement and those that cause long-term conflict and the total breakdown of a relationship. Distinguish too between quarrels or conflicts that happen between close friends or relatives and those that happen between casual acquaintances. Help them to think about differences in response, and in attitude. Ask the children if they think that disagreements between individuals can cause problems within a team, and how far-reaching these problems might be.

Learning objectives
● Understand that some conflict within teams is inevitable.
● Learn about different strategies to cope with and resolve conflict.

Lesson organisation
Teacher introduction and pair work; teacher-led whole-class discussion; group activity; plenary.

CHAPTER 1
BUILDING HEALTHY RELATIONSHIPS

Building a team

Vocabulary
conflict
disagreement
quarrels
solution
negotiation
communication
relationships
acquaintance
coping
stress
argument

As an initial stimulus, divide the class into pairs and get them to try to assess, based on their most recent experiences, whether it is actions or words that are most often the cause of conflicts. Ask some pairs to provide an example of each, encouraging them to give examples of conflicts within teams, if they have recorded any. Use the prepared charts to act as a stimulus to their discussion.

Discuss the kinds of things that are said and help the children to think about classifying these under topics such as: lies about me; criticism of me; calling me names; criticising my friends; bossing me about; not giving me a fair turn. Give the children the opportunity to record the discussion, in their own words, on the appropriate charts.

Discuss other things that are done to cause conflict, such as taking things that don't belong to you; causing physical hurt; ignoring someone.

Again, give the children time to record their opinions and feelings on the charts.

20 mins **Development**

Put two pairs together to make groups of four and give a copy of photocopiable page 110 to each group. Invite them to look at the pictures and make their responses to the statements. Then ask two groups to work together by comparing differences.

Provide other examples of conflict for the children and try to draw out the main courses of action possible to deal with it, such as ignoring it; discussing it; telling someone else about what happened; trying to find ways to bring the other person around to your point of view; asking a friend for advice, and so on.

15 mins **Plenary**

Summarise the causes of conflict with the children. Ask: *Which is the most difficult form of conflict or disagreement to cope with?* Talk about the differences between a discussion, an argument and a conflict. What do they perceive the differences to be?

Ask the children if they think that conflict between members of a team is inevitable. How would they go about resolving it? Discuss any advantages or benefits that might come from a conflict that has been successfully resolved. Have they experience of any such benefits from disagreements with friends or are all their experiences negative? Discuss the idea of winning and losing in terms of conflicts and disagreements. If appropriate, you could develop the discussion to talk about the use of violence to try to resolve conflict. Point out that some political groups try this strategy. Ask the children: *Does it work?*

Differentiation

Less able children will see conflict very much as a physical idea and will think in terms of hitting, or fighting – help them to think beyond this. Encourage more able children to explain and describe a conflict in terms of ideas or opinions as well as what is said.

Provide some key words, such as jealousy, greed or ambition, to help less able children think of reasons for conflict beyond simple likes or dislikes. Ask more able children to identify, and give examples of, beliefs or values.

Assessing learning outcomes

Can the children distinguish between discussion, argument and conflict? Can they distinguish between actions and words as causes of conflict? Can the children reason the possible solutions to conflict, such as: engage with it; avoid it; negotiate; seek help; go it alone? Are they able to articulate their feelings and emotions to such confrontations, such as: *I don't like it; It makes me unhappy; I feel resentful*?

ICT opportunities
Write a poem or newspaper article about a particular conflict on the computer. The children could use the Internet to find an example of a current legal, military, social or political conflict.

Building a nation

At this stage in their intellectual and social development, the children will have begun to encounter and study the characteristic features of other countries. They will be becoming aware of the physical nature, size and location of other countries, as well as their varied cultural heritage and possibly their associated beliefs and value systems. They may have come across these as part of a project linked to geography, history, art or music within the curriculum. You may even have links with a school in another country. Through the media the children should have encountered the fact that Scotland and Wales now have independent forms of government. The issues of Northern Ireland are also likely to be familiar.

At this age the children will also be travelling to other countries on holiday or be meeting people from other countries when they visit Britain. They will begin to be sensitive to differences, initially to language, food, clothes and music. Later the differences may extend to ideas or attitudes towards certain behaviour. Children will not always be so aware of what many of these cultures have in common, and this unit attempts to give them some basic tools for exploring these ideas and attitudes towards nationality and race.

The first activity looks at how a nation is defined. It introduces the idea of simple boundaries, the tangible and intangible 'lines' that define a nation and considers how helpful or unhelpful they can be. The second develops this to examine the idea that, although one may talk of a 'nation' as a single entity, it is, in fact, comprised of many different types of people, all of whom display significant differences in knowledge, skills and values.

The next activity examines the idea of 'image' and how people often build up pictures and make judgements about other people on very limited experience. It also introduces the ideas of prejudice and discrimination.

The final two activities define and describe the idea of a 'healthy' or 'unhealthy' nation and help children to identify criteria by which this assessment can be made, then explore laws and rule-making as they might apply to a nation, examining the processes of negotiation and discussion.

For the teacher, the important task is to get the children to draw on their own experiences, reflect on their own and others' behaviour, assess their feelings and emotions and draw conclusions about the importance of 'nationality' as a concept. There are, within some of the activities, opportunities to explore the more sensitive areas of these topics and concepts like race, prejudice, discrimination and bias will emerge naturally during open discussions of nationality.

Be aware of and sensitive to how your pupils will cope with the expression of such views. It is clearly necessary to allow some children the freedom to say things that represent what they think (or have heard) yet which might be hurtful or insensitive to others. However, this will need to be balanced against the need and desire to protect vulnerable children from being the object of those opinions.

Unit: Building a nation

Enquiry questions	Learning objectives	Teaching activities	Further teaching activities	Learning outcomes	Cross-curricular links
What defines and determines a nation? What types of boundaries are created by nations?	● Understand that a nation can be defined by certain physical 'boundaries'. ● Know that other non-physical 'boundaries' can also define a nation.	Discuss boundaries and the reasons for them. Consider other forms of boundaries, how they affect our judgement and how fair this is.	● Produce a diagram to show how 'boundaries' apply in school or at home. ● Write a letter to a local politician explaining how, as an individual, a particular 'boundary' has affected you. ● Write a letter to someone in a school in another country explaining how different types of boundaries affect your life and asking how they affect theirs.	*Children:* ● understand the use of the term 'boundary' in both its tangible and less tangible senses ● appreciate the reasons why 'boundaries' change and the reasons for those changes ● understand the importance that some people attach to certain boundaries	Geography: using maps and finding boundaries; comparing and contrasting different countries.
What types of groupings exist within a nation? What do such groupings contribute to a nation?	● Be aware that a nation is made up of many different groups of people.	Talk about different groups within a community. Consider and identify positive and negative aspects of having different groups within a community.	● Role-play a situation with a particular group of people who feel that their interests are not being looked after and wish to present their grievances to someone in authority. ● Choose one group of people that has been discussed in class. Design a leaflet to explain the value of that group to the community.	● understand the key idea of a nation being made up of many different groups ● appreciate that the formation of groups of people within a community can be a good or a bad thing ● understand what causes disagreements between groups ● offer reasons for those situations	Geography: using a map of the British Isles; investigating different groups in a community.
How are images and judgements about a nation formed? Are these judgements usually well-founded?	● Understand that people form opinions of others based on many different pieces of evidence. ● Appreciate that these opinions are often based on insufficient evidence.	Discuss how opinions are formed and whether quickly-made judgements are fair. Record ideas on how an overseas visitor would view the children's home town.	● Collect pictures and photographs from brochures and newspapers of places and/or people and describe what 'image' they are portraying to others. ● Write a description of someone famous and challenge the other children to guess who it is.	● understand and appreciate the idea that people may be judged on very flimsy, inadequate information ● comment on the fairness and importance, or otherwise, of such judgements	English: examining pictures and recording ideas.
What is meant by the term, 'unhealthy nation'? What remedies can be found for some of the 'unhealthy conditions'?	● Know that many different factors contribute to the 'health' of a particular environment, and nation as a whole. ● Understand that some of the 'unhealthy' factors are not easy to cure.	Investigate the school environment in small groups, looking for positive and negative points. Think of ways to remedy any unhealthy conditions.	● Apply the idea of 'healthy' and 'unhealthy' to aspects of the school. ● Write an explanation of their work to someone in another country, providing ideas for carrying out a similar investigation. ● Look for articles or events in newspapers related to the 'health' of the nation.	● understand the concept of 'health' as it applies to a nation ● think of the country as 'healthy' ● identify possible solutions to the problems	Health education: definitions and terms related to 'illness'.
How are laws governing a nation established? How does a government ensure that these laws are accepted and upheld?	● Understand that establishing the laws for a nation is a complex process. ● Appreciate that negotiation, compromise and co-operation are part of establishing laws.	In role-play as Government, Opposition, and other Parliamentary roles, debate a new law and take a vote on it.	● Carry out a referendum in school about some particular rule. ● Prepare a 'party political broadcast' for TV in support of a new law. ● Prepare a statement by a 'minority' party expressing dissatisfaction with the government not allowing minority parties to have an adequate voice.	● identify a possible law ● express feelings about the process ● appreciate the wider implications of the process and relate this to how a local council or government might operate.	English: speaking and listening: role-playing a political debate.

1 hour What defines and determines a nation?

What you need and preparation

Cut out shapes of particular countries such as the UK, Italy, South America or Australia. Include some countries without a coastline, perhaps Switzerland or Austria.

You will need several sets of cards – some labelled with single words written in the languages of your selected countries and others with labels that state their currency, such as the euro or dollar. You will also need cards that show the flags, national emblems or national costumes of those particular countries. Keep one set of cards blank.

Provide writing and drawing materials. You will need access to a board or flipchart.

What to do

10 mins Introduction

Introduce the key idea of a boundary as something that defines an area, space or country. Ask the children: *How many different words can you associate with boundary to describe how the word is used?* The children may suggest: *fence, ropes, boards, walls, stones* or *pegs.* Make some suggestions yourself if they do not have many ideas.

Now ask the children: *What kinds of things is a boundary built to do?* Use the example of the border of a country or lines on a sports pitch to explain the idea. Point out that countries have different kinds of boundaries that help to define them as individual nations: seas, mountains, rivers and walls (some of the children may be aware of Hadrian's Wall). Use the cut-out shapes of countries to develop this part of the discussion. Ask the children to identify the shapes, and name the countries.

35 mins Development

Suggest that there are other 'features' that define a nation, such as money or language, although these 'features' may be subject to change.

Play a word association game with the children to develop this idea. Select, or allow one of the children to select, a country, and ask the other children to suggest a word that they associate with that country. Record these on the board and ask the children: *How do you know these words are associated with that country?* Challenge them to justify their suggestions and say if they are fair and reasonable. This game will demonstrate differentiation in the nature and range of the words and ideas introduced. Add words yourself to extend the concept. Look together at the full list of features identified as forming part of that nation. Repeat this several times with different countries.

Now divide the class into groups, allocating each group one of the countries for which you collected information for the labelled cards you prepared earlier. Give each group a small mixed pile of these cards, making sure that each group has cards representing a number of countries and at least one blank card. Explain that each of the words or images on the cards is a kind of

Learning objectives
● Understand that a nation can be defined by certain physical 'boundaries'.
● Know that other non-physical 'boundaries' can also define a nation.

Lesson organisation
Initial teacher introduction and stimulus activity followed by a teacher-led discussion; group activity and discussion; plenary.

Vocabulary
boundary
government
currency
culture
nationality
language
discrimination
prejudice
physical
borders
identity
pride
religion
emblem
race

Building a nation

ICT opportunities
Look for maps of countries, examples of particular languages and information about currency on the Internet.

Follow-up activity
Ask the children to think of boundaries in the sense of things that have limited people's ability to do things. They could develop a timeline on themes such as: *Distance was a boundary until…*; *Communication was a boundary until…* ; *Language was a boundary until…* ; *Space was a boundary until…* .

'boundary' because it helps to define a particular country – it may be a word from its language, its national emblem or dress, or its currency, or something to described its culture, religion or ethnicity.

Explain that each group has to build the identity of one nation by trading or swapping cards with other groups. Suggest that, once the groups have completed the task, they should draw on the blank card one other 'feature' that they think helps to identify that nation. Keep the children aware of the dangers of stereotyping and ask them to justify any unreasonable or old-fashioned assumptions.

15 mins **Plenary**
Discuss with the children the reasons why some people are very proud of their nationality and others don't seem to care. Discuss whether boundaries help or hinder people from getting to know each other better.

Talk with the children about how many boundaries change – they may be changed by governments, currency may change, the language may develop and alter, new people may arrive and add their culture to the existing ones. Discuss the reasons why these changes happen and how people react to them. Encourage them to think of a change that has taken place, or is likely to take place, in Great Britain and ask how people feel about it.

Ask the children how easy they have found it to describe the culture, religion and ethnicity of a country. Did they find them to be more complex than they had first imagined?

Differentiation

Less able children will require help to understand the tangible, and less tangible, elements of a boundary. They may be helped with visual clues, such as a passport or a map.

Encourage more able children to introduce race, colour, or religion into the discussion of boundaries that define a nation.

Assessing learning outcomes

Do the children understand the use of the term 'boundary' in both its tangible and less tangible senses? Do they appreciate the reasons why 'boundaries' change, and the reasons for those changes? Do they understand the importance that some people attach to certain boundaries?

(1 hour) What types of groupings exist within a nation?

Learning objective
Be aware that a nation is made up of many different groups of people.

Lesson organisation
Teacher introduction and initial stimulus activity; teacher-led whole-class discussion; group activities and plenary.

What you need and preparation

Make a copy of photocopiable page 111 for each child. You will need sticky labels and large sheets of paper on which the children can record their work. You will also need photocopiable page 112 – enough for one for each group in the class – and writing materials.

What to do

25 mins **Introduction**
Talk to the children, suggesting that, although we call ourselves British (or French or German), a nation is made up of many different groups of people. We all use labels to distinguish particular groups. *Have you heard people talk about 'Northerners', 'Southerners', the 'rich', the 'poor', the 'middle class', the 'working class'?* Explain that, over time, people within a country have reasons to move or relocate and that this creates a mix. Ask the children: *What reasons do you think people have to move around?*

Divide the class into six groups and give each group of children a large piece of paper. Ask two groups of children: *How many different groups or sets of children can you create from your group?* Two other groups could use the class and another two groups could use the school as their base. Ask the children to write down their 'group' headings on the sheet, for example: this group is good at maths; this group come to school by car; this group enjoy going to the cinema. When they have completed the task, ask them: *What does this show us about our school?* Move on to develop the idea that the existence of groups within a school (or village or town) is often a good thing – the different groups can work together, help each other, help the school. Then ask the children:

● What are the disadvantages of having different groups in a school?
● What things may happen between different groups that are not so good and why do you think these happen?

Conclude the discussion by considering that when groups form, either in a school or community, there may be positive or negative outcomes.

Give each child a copy of photocopiable page 111 and ask them to build up a picture of different groups in their community and the links between these groups. Are these links positive or negative ones?

⏱ **Development**

Give each group the map of the British Isles on photocopiable page 112. Ask the children to mark on their map as many different groups of people in Britain as they can. You might give each group a different set of clues to the possible answers by providing them with key words, such as age, work, religion, nationality and money. The children could then develop a description of that group.

Discuss with the children the idea that some groups of people feel that they are separate, although part of a nation. Ask: *What kinds of things can divide or split groups of people in a nation?*

⏱ **Plenary**

How many groups have the children been able to think of? Ask each group to report on, and explain, two or three of their descriptions. Encourage the class to discuss their impressions of the diverse groups in Britain.

Differentiation

Less able children will need help with the 'map' activity and will require simpler and more specific word clues.

Assessing learning outcomes

Do the children understand the key idea of a nation being made up of many different groups? Can they appreciate that the formation of groups of people within one community can be a good or bad thing? Are the children able to understand what causes disagreements between groups? Can they offer reasons for those situations?

Vocabulary
culture
values
beliefs
symbols
language
heritage
nationality
community
similarity
difference
unique
interest groups

Follow-up activity
Ask the children to describe their village or town through the eyes of a stranger visiting from another country. What might seem strange or curious? What might they not understand? What might they find funny, sad or alarming about the groups of people they meet?

CHAPTER 1
BUILDING HEALTHY RELATIONSHIPS

Building a nation

① How are images and judgements about a nation formed?

Learning objectives
● Understand that people form opinions of others based on many different pieces of evidence.
● Appreciate that these opinions are often based on insufficient evidence.

Lesson organisation
Initial stimulus activity with follow-up; teacher-led discussion; group and paired activities; individual work then pair work; plenary.

Vocabulary
image
judgement
evidence
behaviour
opinions
reputation
accurate
expression
body language
prejudice
values
label

What you need and preparation
Make a collection of photographs or drawings of people with a variety of expressions and stances. These can be of individuals or pairs of people and must have a reasonable close-up of the faces. Make a copy of photocopiable page 113 for each child. Provide writing materials.

What to do

㉕ Introduction
Tell the children that people often form very quick judgements and opinions about other people based on inadequate information and evidence. They may look at the way others dress or eat, how they talk or what they talk about, and then form a judgement about them. Ask the children: *Have you ever done this yourselves? On what did you base your judgements?*

Divide the children into groups and give them one or two of the pictures of people. Ask them to describe the facial expressions: *What sorts of feelings are they showing? Why do you think this?* Ask the children to record any differences of opinion in the group for later discussion.

Now ask the groups to show the pictures or drawings they have been looking at to the other groups in turn. They should describe what they think and check if the other groups agree.

Finish this part of the lesson by asking the children, in their groups, to work on their own representation of a feeling or mood. They should rehearse this and then demonstrate it to the rest of the class. Ask the other groups to guess what sort of feeling or mood is being displayed: *How do you know? How easy was it to decide?*

⑮ Development
Introduce the idea that we may form quick opinions of other nations or countries in much the same way, and that sometimes these can be quite unfair. Ask the children: *How do we form these opinions of other nations or countries?* Suggest that it may be because of the influence of television, or an incident on holiday.

Organise the children into pairs or fours and ask them to imagine that they come from another country and are visiting Britain for only two days. As they have so little time they will only manage to see the town where the children live. What would these visitors report back about Britain to people at home? Ask the children:
● How accurate a picture of Britain would they get from our home town?
● What would they describe as good?
● What would they not like?
Discuss the idea of 'image' with particular reference to a town's 'image'. Ask them:
● What is an 'image' and what does it depend on?
● What 'image' does your school, town or area have?
● How important is it to have a good 'image'?
Give each of the children a copy of photocopiable page 113, ask them to record their ideas and then discuss these with a partner.

⑳ Plenary
Once the sheets and discussion have been completed ask the children how they would feel about the idea of someone making a judgement, or forming an opinion of them, based on a very brief meeting. This may not bother some of the children, but others may not like the idea. Encourage the children to talk about any occasions when a quick judgement might be made which would have serious consequences.

Differentiation

The less able children may need prompts to express opinions, particularly positive ones, on their home town. Suggest that they consider places to see, things to do, special events or special people. Encourage the more able children to provide a comparison with other places they have visited.

Assessing learning outcomes

Do the children understand and appreciate the idea that people may be judged on very flimsy, inadequate information? Are they able to comment on the fairness and importance, or otherwise, of such judgements?

ICT opportunities
Ask the children to draw faces expressing emotions on the computer. They can then explain the expression they are representing.

Follow-up activities
● Invite someone from the town council, Tourist Board, or a business person to talk to the children about 'image', what things contribute to it and why it is important.
● The children could think of ways in which the school 'image' could be improved.

(1 hour) What is meant by the term 'unhealthy nation'?

What you need and preparation

Make a few copies of photocopiable page 114 to use as a stimulus. Provide writing materials.

What to do

(25 mins) Introduction

Introduce the idea that, just like a person, a nation can be healthy or unhealthy. Just as people get sick from time to time, a nation can too. Ask the children what they think it would mean if they read in a newspaper about a 'sick nation'. If the children are unclear what this means then provide some examples by talking about crimes such as burglary or assault, irresponsible behaviour, or of damage done by people to the environment. Ask: *Why do we have organisations such as the NSPCC, RSPCA or RSPB?* (They all offer some sort of protection.) Hand out copies of photocopiable page 114 and use these as a stimulus to the discussion.

(20 mins) Development

Divide the children into small groups and give each group an area of the school to examine: for example the classroom, cloakroom, corridors, school building or immediate surroundings. Tell them that they should examine their area and list any positive or negative points about it. Provide each group with a clipboard, paper and pencils.

Back in the classroom, ask the children to look at their list of points and come up with either a solution to any problems or a suggestion on how to keep any positive points remaining positive. The children might want to think up some class rules about how these areas are treated in future.

Bring the class together and encourage the children to talk about possible remedies for any 'unhealthy' conditions they have been discussing. Discuss any school rules that they have come up with.

(15 mins) Plenary

Extend the discussion of 'healthy' and 'unhealthy' to consider how the terms could be applied to the children's locality. Using photocopiable page 114 as a stimulus, ask the children how they would remedy unhealthy aspects of the environment and protect the healthy areas.

Introduce the idea of responsibility by asking the children: *Who has the responsibility of*

Learning objectives
● Know that many different factors contribute to the 'health' of a particular environment and nation as a whole.
● Understand that some of the 'unhealthy' factors are not easy to cure.

Lesson organisation
Initial teacher introduction and stimulus activity with follow-up, teacher-led discussion; group activities; plenary.

Vocabulary
healthy
unhealthy
illness
condition
responsibility
remedy
cure
frustrated
economic
social
environmental
divide

Building a nation

trying to make the world around us better? Who looks after and improves our environment? Who are the 'doctors' and 'nurses' who can do this? Encourage them to think about the roles of the government, the local council, teachers and parents.

Round up by asking the children to think about what might happen if nothing is done to improve the condition.

Differentiation
The less able children will need help to identify the concept of 'unhealthy'. Some will take the word 'unhealthy' literally and list obvious physical illnesses. Give them pictures or words to extend their ideas.

Others, who are more able, will identify economic, social and environmental illnesses.

Assessing learning outcomes
To what extent do the children understand the concept of a 'health' as it applies to a nation? To what extent are they able to think of the country as 'healthy'? Can they identify possible solutions?

1 hour How are laws governing a nation established?

Learning objectives
● Understand that establishing the laws for a nation is a complex process.
● Appreciate that negotiation, compromise and co-operation are part of establishing laws.

Lesson organisation
Initial teacher-led introduction; group activity; plenary.

Vocabulary
laws
rules
government
election
parliament
argument
debate
party
minority
opposition

What you need and preparation
Produce a short set of rules for debating. These might include: limiting the length of time a person is allowed to speak; setting up a procedure for getting your speech heard; permitting only one person to speak at a time and following the instructions of the 'speaker' of the parliament on behaviour in the debate.

Prepare two briefs – one for each half of the class. The brief for Group 1 is: *you are the party in government and have just won a General Election. You have to decide on one particular law that you want to get passed. You have ten minutes to decide what that law is.* The brief for Group 2 is: *you are the party in opposition – you have just lost a General Election. In ten minutes' time, the Government will inform you of a law which they propose to try to pass. As you are the Opposition you will have to oppose some parts, if not all, of this law.*

Both the rules and the briefs could be written on a board or flipchart or be displayed in other ways. Try to obtain a brief video extract (if possible) of a parliamentary session. Make two copies of photocopiable page 115. You will also need voting slips and writing materials.

What to do
25 mins Introduction
If you have a video clip of a parliamentary session show it to the children before dividing them into two or more groups, depending on the size of the class. Explain that Group 1 is the Government and Group 2 is the Opposition (other groups can be other parties). Nominate two children to be neutral observers. Give Groups 1 and 2 their briefs, then ask Group 1 (the Government) to decide on a law that they think is important and they want to get passed quickly. They will probably need help to make a quick decision. Help them by putting up some ideas on the board – this could be one of the rules the children suggested in the previous lesson, on page 21. Limit their thinking time to ten minutes, then pass the details of the law to Group 2.

While Group 2 are examining these details, encourage Group 1 to appoint two or three speakers to present their law, each taking a different emphasis. They should also prepare their

arguments for wanting to pass it. Limit this decision time to 15 minutes. During this time Group 2 also need to appoint 'speakers' from their members and prepare their opposition arguments.

Set up the classroom as a parliament. Appoint a 'speaker' or act in that role yourself. Realistically you will probably need to have a slight majority on the side of the Government. If you do have other parties you could make these minority parties to make the concept of 'opposition' more complex. Use the list of rules for debating to remind the children about procedures.

25 mins Development

Give the two neutral observers a copy of photocopiable page 115 each. Explain what they have to do and give them time to prepare their recording sheets.

Ask the two groups to debate the law. Start with a brief initial statement from the Government (only allow one or two minutes for this) then a response from the Opposition. Invite the Government speakers to respond or develop their argument and allow other speakers to join in appropriately.

Allow five minutes at the end for a vote to take place. You will need to discuss people's freedom to vote, as members of Group 1 may all vote for the motion and members of Group 2 may vote against it. If other parties have been created then the voting should be more interesting.

10 mins Plenary

Discuss with the children what they learned from the process. Ask them:
● How easy was it to get your view across in a short time?
● Did you put your argument across clearly, do you think other people were listening?

Ask the children to discuss their feelings about the process. Did they feel contented or frustrated with how the 'debate' went? Did they resent others arguing with them or did they enjoy the process of debating? Did they view it as simply trying to win?

Ask the neutral observers to refer to their recording sheets to provide feedback on the process of the debate.

Link the activity to the process of democracy. Do the children think this is a good way to run the country? Discuss the concepts of negotiation and compromise.

Differentiation

The children will need help to identify possible laws for consideration. The less able will focus on school or their own interests, but others may be able to propose wider, community-focused laws. A picture or word stimulus will help the discussion.

Children will need help to develop their cases for or against the law. The less able will relate this only to how the law applies to them, others will be able to justify ideas on the grounds of the 'greater good'. Use prompt cards to develop both perspectives.

Assessing learning outcomes

Are the children able to identify a possible law with relative ease or do they require considerable help? Are they able to relate it to personal experience? Can the children adequately express their feelings about the process? Can they appreciate the wider implications of the process and relate this to how a council or government might operate?

ICT opportunities
The children in each party could produce their response to the law for an imaginary website, perhaps using a website DTP program.

Follow-up activity
Draw up and illustrate a set of rules for younger children to help them learn about how to debate a topic. It could use cartoons and humour.

CHAPTER 2

Building healthy bodies

This chapter explores the all-important area of children's health. It investigates the development of behaviours and attitudes that will ensure that they grow up respecting their bodies (and minds) and adopting a healthy lifestyle. In order to achieve this goal, it is important that the children, from an early age, understand and appreciate how their body works and what they can do to ensure that it continues to work efficiently.

As they grow physically, their knowledge and awareness also has to grow if they are to make decisions about how to treat their bodies and be clear about the implications and consequences of those decisions.

As they mature, the children will also become aware of the pressures of 'healthy living' exerted on them from other areas. Sometimes, these pressures may be 'healthy' – encouragement to take exercise, advice on what to eat and not to eat, suggestions on how to relax and cope with stress. At other times, the pressures will be of a different nature and may be less beneficial, even harmful. They are likely to experience pressure to experiment with substances and take risks by adopting behaviours that could be dangerous.

They will also begin to realise that these pressures will come from a wide variety of contexts. Some will be familiar – friends, acquaintances, maybe even family, while others will be less familiar, perhaps the media or influential groups of people. These less familiar pressures will often have powerful persuasive powers.

There are a number of balances that have to be achieved in this particular area of children's social development – none of which are easy to reach! Firstly, a balance has to be struck between being overly negative and failing to stress the positive ideas and attitudes of healthy living. It is important to avoid the danger of always 'playing up' the worrying elements of the subject. There is also a balance to be achieved between allowing children to reach their own, informed, decisions and simply telling them, being over-prescriptive, even dogmatic. A final balance must be reached between differing values and opinions – respecting personal belief systems that can conflict with each other – school and home, or home and community.

Contexts and developing awareness

This chapter uses a variety of contexts to explore these ideas and attitudes. Some of these will be familiar to the children and ones to which they can readily relate – eating choices, taking exercise, sport. Other contexts will, at least to some children, be less familiar, yet nevertheless very important.

It is important when teaching these elements to put them into a context suitable for the age and ability of the children. For the younger age range, supporting the growing awareness of their behaviour, how they work, and what helps them to work well should be a priority. Individual and paired activities to increase and enhance this awareness are at the core of this aim. With the older age range, where growing independence results in children taking more decisions about their health and exercise, food and leisure activities become the focus. Finally, with the top age range, the whole topic is expanded to look at the wider influences and pressures on children to adopt certain behaviours that are presented as beneficial.

A healthy choice

At this age, children are growing more independent. Some children will be becoming increasingly aware of this and may attempt to exploit the fact in their relationships. They may be given advantage of opportunities to make decisions for themselves. Their decisions will often be based on information and sound judgement, but occasionally they may be based on feelings, emotions, social pressures and a desire to conform and be a part of the group, to be 'grown-up'.

The desire that many children show to explore, experiment, even take risks, grows with this sense of independence. While it is important to recognise some of the positive aspects of this freedom – the desire to try 'new things' and the confidence that it brings when it is accompanied by success – it is also necessary to highlight that there are potential hazards to be faced and overcome.

One important goal, therefore, is to ensure that children know and understand the critical areas of human behaviour in making choices for healthy living. Information is essential for good decision-making – the poorer the information, the less effective the choice. It also supports attitude formation and the building of sound judgements.

The second important goal is to equip the children with skills that they can utilise in situations where sound judgement and a personal response is required. They need to be able to assess information and arguments, and to calculate the 'risk effect'. They also need to be able to analyse and distinguish between fact and fiction, between evidence and opinion. They should also know how to argue a point of view. Finally, they need to be able to use social skills, such as negotiation.

This unit provides opportunities for children to develop these competencies by dealing with the attitudes and pressures behind the desire to take risks and experiment. It provides the children with opportunities to develop the skills to cope with experiences that relate to these issues.

The unit also encourages the children to assess the impact of their behaviour on themselves and others and shows them that coping with the pressure to conform is often difficult and that remaining in control and staying positive are essential skills.

Assessing the claims and persuasive arguments used by others, whether face-to-face or in the media is another important skill that children require and this is also covered. The final lesson in this section looks at the impact of campaigns and pressure groups on people's behaviour and considers the idea of presenting a more positive approach to healthy living.

Unit: A healthy choice

Enquiry questions	Learning objectives	Teaching activities	Further teaching activities	Learning outcomes	Cross-curricular links
What is risk? Is it worth taking risks?	● Understand that making choices often involves taking a risk. ● Appreciate that different activities carry different levels of risk.	Discuss different risks and how they can be graded. Assess levels of risk and consider whether taking risks is ever worthwhile.	● Devise a slogan for a TV commercial which warns of the danger of taking unnecessary risks. ● Devise an interview to do with someone who is a 'high risk taker'. ● Devise a 'risk assessment scale' for a dangerous activity.	*Children:* ● differentiate and grade high and low risk ● provide a range of reasons for the category chosen ● reason with one another and appreciate differences of opinion ● associate everyday events with the element of risk ● understand the idea of taking risks and learning	English: ranking activities.
What is harm? Why do people choose to do things that may harm themselves, or others?	● Appreciate that certain behaviour is harmful to oneself and others. ● Understand that harm can be physical or emotional.	Identify and classify types of harm. Draw pictures of people causing 'harm' and discuss why these situations occur.	● Look for stories in newspapers or on television in which someone has inflicted injury on someone else. Discuss the issues. ● Design a scale to measure 'harm done' for a particular behaviour.	● appreciate the different categories of 'harm' ● extend the idea of harm beyond individuals to groups and whole communities ● appreciate and comment on the idea of people choosing to behave in certain ways, even when they know that these are harmful	Health education: taking risks with our bodies. Art: drawing pictures to represent 'harm'.
What is peer-group pressure? What can be done to resist peer-group pressure?	● Understand that there are different ways of responding to peer-group pressure. ● Appreciate that being positive and self-confident earns the respect of others.	Discuss ways of dealing with peer-group pressure. List assertive phrases and use these in a role-play.	● Produce a booklet illustrating the ways of dealing with techniques of persuasion which are unwelcome. ● Get the children to watch and listen for persuasive techniques in advertising on television and record them.	● provide examples of how to react to peer-group pressure and the associated feelings ● express their responses to this pressure both in words and actions ● balance the idea of resisting pressure with the desire to remain popular, or part of a group	Health education: taking care of, and responsibility for, our actions. English: examining persuasive language.
How are people affected by advertising? Do advertisements give a balanced view?	● Appreciate that advertising has a strong influence on some people's behaviour. ● Understand that the language used in advertising may be misleading.	Look at advertisements for healthy living and discuss their claims. Create an 'alternative' advertisement.	● Design an advertisement of their own for a particular product to service using some of the persuasive language identified. ● Draw up their own Advertising Standards dos and don'ts list. ● Design an advertisement for their school using the dos and don'ts list.	● appreciate the power of advertising in terms of influencing people's behaviour ● relate this to their own experiences and make balanced judgements	Health education: understanding media pressure. English: language of advertising; creating own advertisements.
Do advertisements always have the desired effect? How are effective persuasive advertisements created?	● Recognise that people respond to campaigns in different ways. ● Appreciate that people may understand the information provided but choose to ignore it.	Discuss persuasive advertisements and their effect. Create and assess some persuasive literature.	● Write a letter to a particular campaign group to advise them what not to put into advertisement if they wanted to convince people. ● Pick an example of a particularly poor (or design one of your own) poster or leaflet and display it with all the 'bad' features highlighted.	● appreciate that persuading or prohibiting people's behaviour involves more than just telling them not to do something ● carry out an objective evaluation of the literature ● use reasoned arguments in their own 'campaigns' ● identify the reasons why some people chose to ignore information and evidence.	Maths: statistics, 'big' numbers and percentages. English: writing persuasive text. Art and Design: creating posters.

A healthy choice

 1 **What is risk?**
hour

What you need and preparation

For each group prepare a set of cards with pictures of actions on them that would be familiar to the children. These actions could vary from simple, straightforward behaviour such as walking backwards or forwards with your eyes shut to more 'risky' behaviour such as riding two on a bicycle. In preparation for this lesson, you could ask the children themselves to prepare some 'high-risk' and 'low-risk' 'behaviour' statements or, alternatively, draw pictures for the action cards. Each group will also need two larger cards labelled 'Let's try – low risk' and 'Don't try – high risk'. You will also need access to a board or flipchart, copies of photocopiable page 116 and writing materials.

What to do

25 **Introduction**
mins
Introduce the lesson by asking the children to think about the word 'risk' and other words that they associate with it, such as *chance*, *gamble*, *danger* and *excitement*. Classify these words as either positive or negative and write them in appropriately-labelled columns on the board. Ask: *What kind of activities come into your minds when you hear the word 'risk'?* Record their answers on the board, asking some of the children to explain the reasoning behind their suggestions. Then work down the list and ask the children to assess the 'risk' in the activities chosen on a scale of 1–10.

Sort out all their responses into other types or categories – some will be activities, such as *riding my bicycle fast*, others will be feelings, such as *excitement*, *fun*, or *fear*. Look for contrasting feelings in the children's responses – some may express 'excitement', while others may indicate 'fear', though it is unlikely that children would express the latter openly.

Divide the class into groups, give each group a set of the prepared cards with the behaviour actions or statements on them and the two larger cards labelled 'Let's try – low risk' and 'Don't try – high risk'. Explain that each child, in turn, should pick a card, decide whether it is high or low risk, and allocate it to one of the large labelled cards. Other members of the group can challenge their decision or ask for a reason and one child should record the results. Allow the children about eight minutes to do this. After this time, invite two groups to join up and discuss the way they have sorted their cards. Ask them to record any differences.

Discuss any major differences in opinion at the end of 15 minutes. Ask: *Which activities were labelled 'high risk'? Which activities produced the most disagreement?*

20 **Development**
mins
Suggest that in our everyday lives there is always an element of risk and that we can never plan for the unexpected. Give an example, such as: *If the man hadn't slept later than usual, he wouldn't have missed his train and wouldn't have been on the one that crashed.* Invite the children to give other examples.

Continue the discussion by pointing out that when we do things we cannot predict if the outcome is going to be an accident. Then suggest that sometimes we do know and understand that there is a risk attached to what we do. Give some examples such as people who drive too fast, climb mountains, or go hang-gliding. These people know there is a risk, but they try to take action to reduce the risk. There are other occasions when we may not entirely appreciate the full risk of our behaviour.

Organise the children into pairs and give each pair a copy of photocopiable page 116. Ask them to work through the activities, assessing the element of risk.

Learning objectives
● Understand that making choices often involves taking a risk.
● Appreciate that different activities carry different levels of risk.

Lesson organisation
Initial teacher-led discussion; group and paired activities; plenary.

Vocabulary
risk
choice
evidence
facts
influence
pressure
decisions
peer group
resist
overcome

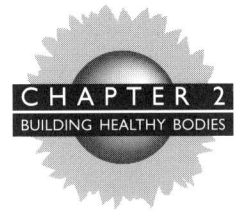

(15 mins) Plenary

Bring the class back together with their photocopiable sheets and ask them to compare their responses.

Discuss why some people like taking risks, perhaps for excitement, to look good, or for gain (as in the case of a burglar). Ask the children if they have heard of anything recently that they would describe as risky and ask them if they think that it is only certain types of people who take risks. Discuss the idea that, 'you only learn by taking risks', in other words that you learn through experience what you can and can't cope with, and what your feelings would be in these circumstances. Suggest that you also learn about how other people cope with risk, and how reliable they are.

Follow-up activities
● Ask the children to develop a board game called 'Risks'. They should think up a basic idea, some risks to encounter and how to play it. Try the game out with other classes.
● Invite the children to think of famous historical or scientific characters who took risks, such as explorers or designers.

Differentiation

Challenge the more able children to think of risks that carry more serious consequences. Can they think of activities that carry consequences for people other than the person doing the activity?

Assessing learning outcomes

Can the children differentiate high and low risk? Can they grade risk between these extremes and provide a range of reasons for the category chosen? Can the children reason with one another and appreciate differences of opinion? Can they associate everyday events with the element of risk? Do they understand the idea of learning through taking risks?

(1 hour) What is harm?

Learning objectives
● Appreciate that certain behaviour is harmful to oneself and others.
● Understand that harm can be physical or emotional.

Lesson organisation
Introductory focus to the lesson and initial teacher-led discussion; group activity and discussion; plenary.

What you need and preparation

Collect some pictures of children and adults engaged in risk-taking activities and try to obtain some posters related to anti-smoking or anti-drinking campaigns. You will need a plentiful supply of blank paper or card on which children can draw, and writing and drawing materials. You may also wish to use the board or flipchart.

What to do

(20 mins) Introduction

Introduce the lesson by asking the children to think of sentences that include the word 'harm'. As they suggest these, try to classify them into types of harm, such as physical, mental or emotional. You might need to record this classification on the board. Initially, the children may not think of emotional or mental harm and you may need to prompt them. Ask: *If someone kept on telling you that you were no good at art, do you think that might be a harmful thing to say?* The word 'hurtful' may also occur in the discussion so be prepared to examine and discuss the two words.

Conclude the initial discussion by suggesting that things we do to ourselves may cause us harm, things that other people do to us may cause us harm and, finally, things that we do to ourselves may cause harm to ourselves and to others.

Vocabulary
harm
hurt
harmful
hurtful
feelings
empty
emotions
sensitive
responsible
caring

(25 mins) Development

Divide the class into groups of six and ask each group to produce three drawings, working in pairs. One pair should produce a drawing that represents someone doing something to cause harm to him or herself, the second pair illustrate a situation of someone causing harm to another person, and the third pair draw a picture to show someone causing harm to themselves and someone else.

The drawings produced by each group of six should then be passed to another group with the instructions to discuss them and answer the question: *What's the harm?* Tell them to answer the question in a series of short sentences that explain the physical, mental or emotional harm caused by the action in the drawing.

After 15 minutes the answers and drawings are passed back to their creators who are then given the opportunity to add more detail to their drawings in the light of what the other group has written.

If time allows, introduce more photographs or pictures that develop the idea of harm into other antisocial behaviour, such as hooligans damaging property, riots or fighting, or a war scene. Alternatively, use posters that discourage smoking and drinking or drugs to widen the discussion on behaviour that is likely to cause harm.

Introduce the topic of the risks some people take when they choose to use drugs. Distinguish with the children the different types of drugs, such as medication, alcohol, cigarettes and illegal substances ('hard' and 'soft' drugs) Some people might even add things like coffee. Bear in mind that, when presenting facts about drugs, it is important to be sure of the facts and make any opinions you express direct and clear. Some children may, at home or in other environments, hear values and opinions expressed that differ from those held by the school and the teacher.

(15 mins) Plenary

Discuss the idea that sometimes people do things that they know could be harmful, yet they still continue. Ask the children why they think people behave like this. Remind them that, at other times, people do things without realising the harm they can cause.

Discuss how far it is reasonable to go in trying to prevent people doing potentially harmful things if they say: *It's not harming anyone else; it's my life, my body.*

Differentiation

Show the less able children specific pictures or photographs to introduce the idea of harm, particularly in terms of how harmful behaviour can affect other people.

Ask the more able children to consider harm that might affect a whole community.

Assessing learning outcomes

Can the children appreciate the categories of 'harm' introduced at the beginning of the lesson? Are they able to extend the idea of harm beyond individuals to groups and whole communities? Can they appreciate and comment on the idea of people choosing to behave in certain ways, even when they know that these are harmful?

Follow-up activities
● Write a script for a scene, a conversation between two people, about someone who has behaved in a way that has caused harm to another person.
● Invite a police or fire officer to come and speak to the children about how they talk to offenders about the harm caused by their behaviour.

A healthy choice

① What is peer-group pressure?
hour

Learning objectives
● Understand that there are different ways of responding to peer-group pressure.
● Appreciate that being positive and self-confident earns the respect of others.

Lesson organisation
Introductory focus to the lesson and initial teacher-led discussion; small group activity; plenary.

What you need and preparation

Make sure that you have access to a board or flipchart, a tape recorder and either a video or 'instant' camera. Make a copy of photocopiable page 117 for each child in the class and provide writing materials.

What to do

30 **Introduction**
mins
Introduce the idea that we may be persuaded by friends or acquaintances to do things that may be risky or harmful, either to ourselves or to others. These people might suggest that we steal something, drink alcohol, or cause damage.

Ask the children to think of any phrases that they have heard used to persuade people to do something, such as: *Come on, don't be a baby!* or *Go on, no one will know!* Write all the suggested phrases on the board. Ask the children if they have ever been asked to do something that they felt was not right. Record their answers on the board. Then hand out the copies of photocopiable page 117 and ask the children to complete the two speech bubbles for each picture.

Once the sheets are completed, tell the children that there are other ways of responding and reacting to this type of pressure. They could take another action, such as walking away. Point out that sometimes this may be the first thing to do, at other times it may be the last resort. They could also consider telling someone else (sometimes this too may be a last resort if other strategies don't work) or try saying something positive to make their point of view and feelings very clear. It is often a good idea to state your opinion clearly at the start of a situation like this to judge how serious the suggestion is. Make clear to the children that it often depends on how well they know the person. If it is someone they don't know, the outcome may not matter, but if it is a friend, it will.

Divide the class into groups of four and give them the following task. Create a scene in which one friend is trying to persuade another to steal some sweets from a shop. One pair should write down all the 'persuading' phrases and the other pair all the possible 'rejection responses'. You may have to provide one or two examples of the latter to get the second group started, such as *I don't want to do that*, *It's not right* and so on. The photocopiable sheet could be used again at this point.

15 **Development**
mins
Ask a few pairs of children to act out their scenes, using the two sets of phrases they have listed. Help them to put emphasis and stress into the phrasing, and encourage them to use body language to emphasise the phrases they are using. Remind them that they can use facial expressions, hands, stance and posture to reinforce their message. Ask other children to give the pairs feedback on the way they are speaking the phrases and their use of body language to depict their meaning.

Vocabulary
pressure
resist
tempting
peer group
self-esteem
confident
react

Use a video recorder or tape recorder and camera to record these exchanges. At the end, ask the children to talk about the feelings they had when they were saying and acting out these phrases.

 15 mins **Plenary**
Discuss with the children why it is not easy to resist the pressure of friends. They may not want to lose a friend or appear a 'baby'. Should they sacrifice a friendship if the pressure becomes too great? Discuss what happens if they reach a stage where they feel they can't cope with the pressure on their own.

Talk about the problems associated with having to tell someone else in confidence about the friend's behaviour. Discuss the options a child would have, in terms of who to tell – a teacher, a parent, another friend or a relation. Although this is a sensitive subject, children generally appreciate that these situations do happen and that they have to deal with them. The message you need to give is to be positive, assertive and self-confident without being aggressive.

Differentiation
You may need to give less able children some of the 'persuading' or 'rejecting' phrases to help their ideas to develop. Show them pictures of people expressing feelings to get across the idea of body language. You could even demonstrate the idea in class.

More able children could explore using more reasoned arguments to counter someone's suggestions.

Assessing learning outcomes
Are the children able to provide examples of how to respond to peer-group pressure and the associated feelings? Are they able to express their responses to this pressure both in words and actions? Can the children balance the idea of resisting pressure with the desire to remain popular or part of a group?

1 hour How are people affected by advertising?

What you need and preparation
Collect sets of advertisements, particularly those related to food, drink and exercise. Prepare a copy of photocopiable page 118 for each child in the class to assess the impact of the sample advertisements. You will also need writing and drawing materials.

What to do
25 mins **Introduction**
Introduce the idea that advertising is about persuading people to behave in certain ways that they are encouraged to believe are good for them. Most adverts are produced by companies who are trying to increase the sale of their product. These adverts often tell people that their lives will be better if they buy a particular new car or computer, or go on a particular 'fantastic' holiday. Ask the children to identify examples of this type of persuasion from food, drink and exercise advertisements that they have seen in magazines or on television. They should be able to offer examples of their own to this discussion, but prompt them by showing them some of your collected advertisements if they do not.

Tell the children that billions of pounds are spent every year on advertising. Ask them: *Does this prove that advertising works if companies are prepared to spend such large sums of money?*

Invite the children to consider what the advertisements discussed previously are claiming

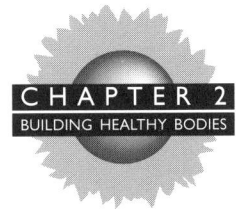

A healthy choice

Vocabulary
persuasion
influence
advertising
promotion
appeal
values
pressure

ICT opportunities
● Children could design 'alternative' advertisements on the computer.
● Some children could look at advertisements on the Internet.

Follow-up activities
● Investigate how much adults are influenced by advertisements related to a healthy lifestyle. Design a questionnaire and record and present the results.
● Invite a local guest speaker to talk about advertising or promoting a product or service aimed at enhancing people's lifestyles – perhaps a health club owner or a food and drinks manufacturer.

to offer people in terms of a healthier lifestyle. Ask them if they think these claims sound truthful and reliable. Emphasise that advertisements are produced according to very strict rules and if it is considered that these rules have been broken (or there are complaints) then the advertisement may be banned. Compare the rating of films in the cinema as a further example.

Move on to discuss the issue of contrasting and conflicting messages in advertising, particularly in terms of a healthy lifestyle. Point out that messages may be contradictory. Use the example of cigarette advertisements which often present a glamorous image, even though they carry a health warning. Ask the children: *Cigarettes and cigarette advertisements carry a health warning – should the same rule be applied to advertisements for alcohol?*

Give each child a copy of photocopiable page 118 and ask them to look at the questions on it in relation to one of the advertisements you have previously discussed or another of their choosing. This should stimulate discussion. Follow up their responses to the questions on the photocopiable sheet, making sure to consider the visual appeal of the advertisements as well as the words. Ask the children if they think that the visual elements are more persuasive than what is written or spoken.

Divide the class into groups of about six and give each group two of the advertisements you have collected for products related to 'healthy living' – food, drink or exercise. Ask them to imagine that they are the panel of judges who have to approve the use of these advertisements in a magazine or on television. Ask them to assess each advertisement – what it says, what it shows, what it claims: *What questions would you ask of the makers of this product?* They can use photocopiable page 118 to help them. Ask them to make a judgement about whether the advertisement is acceptable and write down their conclusion.

Development
20 mins Ask the groups to swap their advertisements and opinions with another group. The second group should discuss and comment on the judgements made for agreement or disagreement.

Now ask the groups to consider the idea of the 'alternative' advertisement. Tell them to imagine that they have been given the opportunity to choose a product (real or imaginary) and have to produce an 'alternative' advertisement that puts across the less favourable, less attractive viewpoint. Point out that they may only tell the truth and should avoid exaggeration. Allow the groups about ten minutes to complete these advertisements, then ask them to pass them around to other groups for comment.

Plenary
15 mins Discuss with them the kinds of things within an advertisement that attract their attention, make them take notice, and might even persuade them to buy a product.

Differentiation
The less able children will need to have a range of advertisements to illustrate the ideas, as they may not find enough material in just one or two. They will also need help with ideas for the 'alternative' advertisement.

More able children could be asked to look for the hidden messages in advertisements, particularly any subtle visual messages.

Assessing learning outcomes
Are the children able to appreciate the power of advertising in terms of influencing people's behaviour? Can they relate it to their own experiences and make judgements? Can they empathise fully with the role of judges and make balanced judgements?

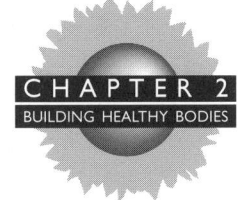

(1 hour) Do advertisements always have the desired effect?

What you need and preparation

Find some examples of advertisements, posters, brochures or leaflets encouraging people to behave, or not behave, in certain ways – these might come from campaigns against smoking, drinking, drugs and speeding. You will also need pictures and photographs linked to these behaviours and writing materials. Make a copy of photocopiable page 119 for each child.

What to do

(25 mins) Introduction

Talk to the children about any advertisements or promotions they see and hear that make them consider how they behave. Suggestions may include advertisements about things to eat and drink, or promotional material for taking exercise, not smoking, taking care on the roads or 'stranger-danger' advice. Begin the discussion by suggesting that a lot of time, energy and money is spent on trying to stop people from doing certain things. Children learn, at an early age, the meaning of words and phrases like: *No! Don't do that! Stop that!* and so on. Encourage the children to think of examples from their own experience of being told not to do certain things. Ask them to say if they felt these instructions were sensible and if they understood why they were being given.

Develop the discussion by showing some examples of advertisements and other literature on topics like road safety, or playing near dangerous places or with electrical equipment. Discuss the reasons why children or adults are encouraged to avoid certain ways of behaving. Suggestions may include their own safety and the safety of others and avoiding irresponsible, immoral or illegal behaviour.

Introduce the idea that in some cases saying *No!* may actually encourage people to rebel and do the opposite. Ask the children to offer suggestions to why this is. They are likely to suggest that some children like to defy rules, and that others may not appreciate the danger.

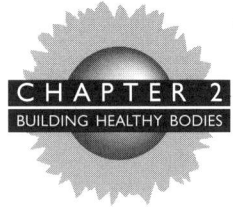

A healthy
choice

Divide the class into small groups and give each group one or two examples of the posters or brochures. Explain that their task is to discuss the content of the posters or leaflets and answer the question: *Would this persuade you not to do this?* Ask the group to provide reasons for their responses. Then ask them for suggestions as to how such a leaflet might be made more persuasive. Point out that some campaigns do more than just describe the consequences, they actually show the consequences in the hope that this will frighten people out of behaving in this way.

Ask groups to pair up, discuss their findings and compare what they have decided. Ask them to identify any messages in the literature that they think are particularly powerful or persuasive and give reasons for their opinions.

(20 mins) Development
Organise the children into groups and ask them to develop their own poster, leaflet, brochure or TV advertisement targeting particular groups of people and particular behaviours. Photocopiable page 119 contains some statistics on road safety that they can use as stimulus for their posters. Some children will be able to identify a suitable subject for their campaign but others may require some help. Suggest topics such as: cigarettes, drugs, litter, vandalism or theft. Encourage the children to use text, visuals and sounds to develop their ideas and remind them to begin by identifying their 'target group' so that the message is specific and precise. If possible, allow the children access to the Internet to find examples of similar campaigns as these may help them form their ideas.

At the end of ten minutes ask one group to present their results to another group, who must provide feedback on impact, appeal, persuasiveness and reality. The two groups can then swap presentation and feedback roles.

(15 mins) Plenary
Sum up and assess the idea of 'No' campaigns. Ask the children why they think it is that people are given information and yet sometimes choose to ignore it: perhaps they don't believe it could happen to them or they don't like being told what to do. Talk to the children about campaigns that use 'positive' rather than 'negative' messages, stressing achievements rather than failures. Ask them if they think this approach has a greater impact.

Differentiation
Less able children will need specific prompts and help to understand concepts such as 'powerful' and 'persuasive'.

Assessing learning outcomes
Do the children appreciate that persuading or prohibiting people from doing things involves more than just telling them not to do it? Are they able to carry out an objective evaluation of the literature? Are the children able to use reasoned arguments in their own campaigns? Are they able to identify the reasons why some people choose to ignore information and evidence?

ICT opportunities
● Carry out research on 'No' campaigns on the Internet.
● Use a simple graphics package on the computer to develop a leaflet or brochure.

Follow-up activities
● Select a problem in school and try to identify ways to get rid of it by encouraging positive behaviour from everyone and discouraging antisocial behaviour.
● Invite a guest speaker who has worked on a campaign to talk to the children about approaches to persuading members of the public.

Healthy exercise

Helping children to develop an understanding of living a healthy lifestyle, taking care of their bodies and dealing with the pressures from all sections of our community, requires exploration of a number of general considerations.

At the heart of this understanding is the issue of how children manage themselves, their time, their knowledge and their skills. This unit encourages the children to think of themselves as managers of their own time, capable of deciding how best to use their resources. It invites them to consider issues such as wasting and prioritising time in the context of living a healthy lifestyle. The children are asked to examine concepts like efficiency and effectiveness as they apply to the use of time and their health.

At this age it is also important that children consider 'health' in a wider context than just their bodies. In this unit children are required to examine the idea of exercising the mind and some of the methods they can use to develop and maintain a healthy mind. They are asked to plan a 'fitness programme' for others to try out and assess its success.

When children (or adults) consider issues of their health and healthy living, one of the most important skills in helping to make decisions is that of assessing the advantages and disadvantages. Children are encouraged to explore costs and benefits – the idea of having to give up or limit some action in order to gain benefits. They also assess the level of cost and gain – an important judgement when choosing a particular course of action.

For some people, healthy living and exercise is found by working for the benefit of others. Such activity not only contributes to the physical health and well-being of the person who helps a neighbour, or the community, but it also enhances the 'health of the mind'.

Finally, the concept of 'learning from exercise' is explored. Learning that is gained in addition to the benefits of developing a healthy body. The children explore how and what they learn about themselves – self-discipline, control, patience and perseverance, as well as what they learn about other people.

The activities are designed for individual children, pairs and small groups. They examine knowledge, behaviour and attitude, promoting discussion and frank exploration of the subject. The role of the teacher is to facilitate the activities, guide discussion, introduce additional material and open up alternative avenues of exploration.

Unit: Healthy exercise

Enquiry questions	Learning objectives	Teaching activities	Further teaching activities	Learning outcomes	Cross-curricular links
In what ways is 'time' a resource? How can time be wasted?	● Understand that it is important to achieve a balance in how time is spent.	Discuss the effective use of time. Analyse and classify their own use of time over one day and then one week and identify healthy activities.	● Design a humorous cartoon and story depicting how time can sometimes be wasted. ● Write the words for a song or poem entitled 'What a waste!'. ● Produce a class newspaper called 'It's time we...'.	*Children:* ● understand and appreciate that time is a resource ● assess a day in terms of effective and non-effective uses of time ● consider the idea of changing how we behave to use time more effectively	Health education: taking time to exercise for our health.
Do we need to exercise our minds? How might we do this?	● Know that exercise can apply to the body and the mind. ● Understand that exercising one can help the other.	Design, record and try out an exercise programme for the mind. Discuss the wider concept of exercise.	● Produce a 90-second radio broadcast to explain 'Exercising the mind'. ● Design a marketing poster to promote the idea of 'mind games'. ● Produce an activity for a friend entitled 'How do you feel about this?'.	● identify with the idea of mental exercise ● think of a variety of activities for the fitness programme ● think of activities related to exercising feelings ● provide feedback on their progress	Health education: keeping fit. Science: fitness and diet.
What are 'costs' and 'benefits'? Are some more significant than others?	● Understand that all decisions have costs and benefits (disadvantages and advantages). ● Appreciate that costs and benefits can relate to health and well-being.	Assess the costs and benefits of different activities and courses of action. Consider how these may affect oneself, and other people.	● Design a cost-benefit chart for use at home with the family. Mark good things that happen as benefits and bad things as costs. ● Produce a range of drawings which would help other children to understand the idea of a 'cost' and a 'benefit'. ● Try the 'benefit chart' in the classroom.	● appreciate the idea of 'costs' relating to things other than money ● appreciate 'benefits' as they apply to a healthy lifestyle ● differentiate between 'low' and 'high' costs and apply them to their behaviour ● appreciate the idea of people benefiting personally from helping others ● put themselves 'in someone else's shoes' and represent their feelings and ideas	English: examining pictures and recording responses to them.
What reasons are there for helping others? Can helping others benefit the helper?	● Appreciate that some people relate 'healthy living' to helping others. ● Understand that costs and benefits can be related to voluntary work.	Discuss how many people benefit by helping others. Create literature and advertisements to encourage people to help others.	● Produce a school newspaper on the theme of 'working for others'. Get stories on what people have done. ● Look for stories in newspapers on the theme of 'working for others' and make a classroom collage. ● Design a set of awards for different levels of activities related to 'working for others'.	● organise themselves effectively to produce their advertisement ● assess their advertisement objectively in relation to a 'professional' product.	English: using persuasive language; writing scripts for advertisements. Drama: acting out advertisements.

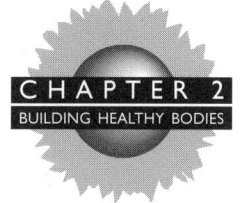
In what ways is 'time' a resource?

What you need and preparation

Make copies of photocopiable pages 120 and 121 for each child. Provide writing materials.

What to do

25 mins Introduction

Introduce to the children the idea of time being a resource (something of which we have a limited amount for our use) like money, water or oil. Point out that it is something we are always using up. Suggest that time is a little different from other resources because we associate the others with money. We have to pay for them and this can make us careful. With time, we don't always think of the cost.

Ask the children to think of other resources and discuss the fact that some of these are non-renewable (they will eventually run out) while others are renewable. Ask the children if they think time is a renewable or non-renewable resource. Offer the phrase *I wish I could have my time over again* and ask them: *What does this phrase mean?*

Introduce the idea that it is possible to waste time, just as we waste water, money or electricity. Ask the children to think of occasions when someone has said to them: *You're wasting your (or my) time.* What were they doing? Do they think the person was right? What criteria would they use to judge whether time was being wasted – perhaps that nothing positive or definite resulted from the use of the time, or that the event was instantly forgotten?

Divide the class into pairs but give each child a copy of the clock on photocopiable page 120. Ask them to think back to yesterday and how they spent their time. Then, individually, they should complete the sheet. Encourage them to be as detailed as possible, emphasising that the point of the exercise is to examine carefully how their time was used. Discuss the view that 'enjoying yourself' or 'having a good time' is sometimes felt to be a waste of time, and reassure them that everyone needs to relax and unwind.

When they have completed this task, ask them to rank the importance of the activities they have recorded. They should give each activity a mark between 1 and 10 depending on how necessary it was to spend time on it (10 is for high priority, 1 for low). Suggest that they discuss their rankings with their partner. At the end of this exercise, ask the pairs to write a statement which assesses how well they used their time during the day. Then put pairs together to compare their assessments.

20 mins Development

Ask the children if they think that time can be divided in other ways, such as: exercising, doing something for other people, thinking about something that has happened, reflecting and planning. Ask if they have heard people using phrases such as: *I spent so much time worrying about my exam* or *I spent so much time telling that person.* These phrases imply that the person thought it was a waste of time! Ask the children if they can think of other categories into which time can be divided.

Divide the class into groups of four and give each member a copy of photocopiable page 121. Explain that they are to analyse their week into 'time spent doing healthy things', filling in the information on the photocopiable sheet. Allow them to interpret the task or, if you feel that they need help, give them some headings to get them started: exercise of various kinds, eating, working. Tell them to try to give a time for each activity. When the sheets have been completed ask them to work out the average time the group spent on healthy activities. Tell them to work out what proportion of time they spent on passive tasks. What proportion of time

Learning objective
Understand that it is important to achieve a balance in how time is spent.

Lesson organisation
Introductory focus to the lesson and initial teacher-led discussion; paired activity; group activity and discussion; plenary.

Vocabulary
choice
balance
managing
allocate
distribute
effective
efficient

did they spend on physically active tasks?

Ask two groups to join together and compare their findings. Based on this they should make an assessment of whether they think their findings show that they are careful about their health.

15 mins Plenary

Ask the children whether they think about how they are using their time when they are doing something: *At the end of playing, working, watching TV, or using the computer, do you ever think that was not a good use of the time?* Ask them to complete the phrase *I would have been better off doing...*

Talk to the children about whether they ever think about changing how much time they spend doing things. Introduce the term 'effective' to describe making good use of their time and ask them how they feel when other people accuse them of wasting their time: *Does it make you think about it, or just make you annoyed?* How do they think other people would feel if they said it to them?

Differentiation

The less able children will need guidance to achieve sufficient detail in the diary exercise. Offer them some headings to help them get started. Photographs or drawings might also help the less able children to categorise time in other ways.

Assessing learning outcomes

Do the children understand and appreciate that time is a resource? Do they attach importance to how they use their time? Are they able to assess their day in terms of effective and non-effective uses of time? Are the children able to consider the idea of changing how they behave to use their time more effectively?

ICT opportunities
Children could collate the data from the photocopiable sheets on the computer.

Follow-up activities
● Develop some poems on the theme of time and how it is used.
● Design posters for the school that encourage other children to think about how they use their time.

① Do we need to exercise our minds?

What you need and preparation

The children will need recording sheets that list the days and hours of the week. They will also need writing materials. Make a copy of photocopiable page 122 for each child. Collect photographs and pictures of a range of 'exercising' activities, both physical and mental.

What to do

㉕ Introduction

Explain to the children that when we speak of exercise we tend to think only of physical exercise, sport and recreational activities for the body such as jogging, aerobics or football. Emphasise that this kind of exercise is important and that everyone needs to find time to take exercise in order to keep healthy.

Invite the children to identify the ways in which they take exercise – at school, at home, or at a sports club or leisure centre. They can refer back to their earlier data collection exercise in the last activity on page 37. Ask the children for their thoughts on the different kinds of motivation that may be behind taking exercise – the urge to keep fit and healthy, looking good, being able to compete well at sports, joining in with friends or developing new skills. If they do not suggest these then offer some ideas yourself.

Introduce the idea that 'taking exercise' can be applied to other areas of our development. The children may have heard people talk about 'exercising your brain' or 'exercising your mind'. Give each child a copy of photocopiable page 122 and use this to discuss this wider concept of exercise. Then ask the children to complete the sheet in pairs or small groups, writing 'Yes' or 'No' beside each picture and to record areas of agreement and disagreement. Get one or two pairs to 'replay' their discussion to the class to give some indication of how the discussion developed.

Now divide the class into groups and set the following task. Tell them that they have to decide on an exercise programme (rather like a fitness programme) for exercising the mind, brain or feelings. They are free to choose the focus of the programme. Encourage them to think of suitable activities themselves, but make suggestions like reading or chess, if children are really stuck. Tell them that each group needs to devise an exercise programme for one week, which would help a person to develop his or her thinking, feeling, or mental health. Encourage them to think of the most suitable activities, give a brief explanation of how to do them, and describe their benefits. They should record their programme on the recording sheet you have prepared, using words and pictures.

⑳ Development

Over the next few days, allocate time for each group to try out one of the exercise programmes designed by another group. They should follow the instructions provided and report back to the group who designed it on its overall effect and their progress. The class could then produce a progress chart for display, identifying the different exercises and their outcomes. Particular exercises could be performed in the class lesson. Refinements to the programme might be suggested and then tried. Other classes could be invited to share the exercise programme and report on their progress.

Learning objectives
● Know that exercise can apply to the body and the mind.
● Understand that exercising one can help the other.

Lesson organisation
Introductory focus to the lesson and initial teacher-led discussion; small group activity; plenary.

Vocabulary
stimulation
mind
body
exercise
development
thinking
ideas
mental
physical
emotional

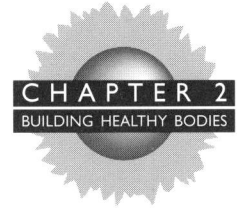

15 mins **Plenary**

Discuss the idea that exercise and enjoyment are two important aspects of healthy living but that sometimes there can be a conflict – some things that people enjoy do not create a healthy lifestyle. Many people enjoy food, or good wine, and some like spending their relaxation time drinking with friends or having meals out. Be careful not to be critical of such activities but simply present them as facts for discussion. Ask the children to look at examples of how these two ideas can conflict.

Discuss the wider concept of 'exercise' to include feelings and emotions: *How do we 'exercise' these? How do we practise developing these parts of our personality?* Within the discussion consider too the dangers or risks attached to the idea of exercising our emotions – as in other forms of physical exercise, people can be hurt or injured. If, for instance, someone says: *I'm going to practise being more honest and forthright with my friends.* How might this result in problems? Or if someone says: *I'm going to be more assertive, I'm not just going to say 'yes' to everything and everyone.* This is 'exercising' one's values and beliefs but it is demonstrated in behaviour. How could this be a problem?

Differentiation

The less able children will need help with ideas for the exercise programme. Give them examples of activities, such as doing a crossword or mental puzzle each day, reading a poem or listening to music.

Encourage the more able children to find interesting variations on the fitness routine.

Assessing learning outcomes

Can the children identify with this idea of exercise? Are they able to think of a variety of activities for the fitness programme? Are they able to think of activities related to exercising feelings? Are they able to provide feedback on progress?

ICT opportunities
Use a graphics package to illustrate the fitness programme on the computer. Include games, quizzes, puzzles and challenges.

Follow-up activity
Extend the programme over time or with other groups. Ask parents to help develop a programme for adults.

---

1 hour ## What are costs and benefits?

What you need and preparation

Collect some pictures of different types of leisure, work and sport activities to use as stimulus for the activities and support for the less able children. Writing and drawing materials will also be required. Make copies of photocopiable pages 123 and 124 for each child.

What to do

25 mins **Introduction**

Discuss with the class the fact that healthy foods are often more expensive than 'junk' food. Discuss with them how the cost or benefit of something does not necessarily equate to money.

Introduce the idea that when we make a decision and choose a certain course of action, there is nearly always a cost, something that we have to give up, lose or turn down. Perhaps to be in the school play we have to attend rehearsals and miss a favourite television programme. Ask the children: *Is this a cost?* Point out that, although cost often means financial cost, in this instance we are not talking about money. Develop one example with the children, such as: *You choose to stay in to watch a football match on television one night – does this have a cost?* Point out that it may do if you fail to finish homework or have to turn down an invitation to go to the cinema to see a new film with friends.

Suggest that, hopefully, there are also benefits from most of the decisions that we make.

Learning objectives
● Understand that all decisions have costs and benefits (disadvantages and advantages).
● Appreciate that costs and benefits can relate to health and well-being.

Lesson organisation
Introductory focus to the lesson and initial teacher-led discussion; paired activity; group activity; plenary.

**Healthy
exercise**

Vocabulary
cost
benefit
opportunity
value
worth
choice
decision
consequences

We may gain things, such as new skills, new knowledge, new friends or new opportunities to travel. Sometimes, those gains will benefit other people as well as ourselves – new skills can often be used to help others. Ask the children: *If you decide to learn to play the piano or learn how to use a computer – how might these new skills help others?* Again, develop an example with the children: *You agree to do some shopping for an elderly relation – what's the benefit?*

Divide the class into groups and give each child copies of both photocopiable sheets. Ask the children to look at the pictures on photocopiable page 123 and record first, in the appropriate column on photocopiable page 124, all the 'costs' they can identify for that person doing that activity. When they have completed this task, they should move on to record the 'benefits', and the complete the other columns, making their personal response in the final column. Once the children have completed the sheets they should discuss their work within the group and then invite other groups to review what they have produced. Encourage them to ask each other questions about the judgements they have made, but ensure that children are given the opportunity to justify their statements.

🕒 Development

Ask the children to think now about the idea of 'costs' to others and 'benefits' to others. Focus particularly on the idea of healthy living and the ways in which 'costs' and 'benefits' relate to this.

Put the children into pairs to play a game of 'Consequences'. Explain that the first child thinks of, and states, an activity, such as: *If I did 20 minutes of exercise every day…*; *If I ate less sweets or crisps…*; *If I cycled to school…*; *If I drank less fizzy drinks…*; *If I ate smaller portions of chips…*; *If I ate more vegetables….* His or her partner has to respond with a consequence, such as: *…that would make you more fit*; *…that would be good for your teeth*; and so on. The game then moves on to the next pair. If any child fails to think of an activity or a consequence, the pair are eliminated.

Now ask the children to draw people exercising, or taking part in what they think are healthy pursuits, and then record the 'costs' and 'benefits' both to the individual and other people. Remind them that both 'costs' and 'benefits' could apply to both the individuals and others.

Allow the children time to explain their drawings and conclusions to other groups. Then, in whole-class discussion, talk about the phrase 'the feel-good factor'. Ask the children if they can see what this might mean in terms of healthy living – *I feel good because I discipline myself to eat less or take exercise. I feel good because I know I am healthy and fit. I feel good because I know I can compete with other people.* Handle this part of the discussion delicately, as it may be a sensitive area for children who feel self-conscious about their weight. It is even possible that some may be the objects of ridicule and bullying.

15 mins **Plenary**
Discuss with the children the idea that 'costs' have to be assessed, and that some costs may be higher than others. Likewise, there are low 'benefits' and high 'benefits'. Discuss the skill of assessing how to judge 'low' and 'high' in this situation. Remind them that what might be a 'healthy' activity for one person and, therefore, a benefit, may be at a 'cost' to another person – perhaps a parent giving up time to run them to football practice. Likewise a 'cost' to the individual may have a 'benefit' for others – giving up time to visit someone who is ill or to learn to use signing to speak to deaf people.

Differentiation
The less able will need some cues to help them with the idea of 'costs' and 'benefits' to others. Use some pictures to introduce the idea.

Assessing learning outcomes
Do the children appreciate the idea of cost relating to things other than money? Are they able to appreciate 'benefits' as they apply to a healthy lifestyle? Can they differentiate between 'low' and 'high' costs and apply them to their behaviour?

ICT opportunities
Children could produce the drawings on the computer.

Follow-up activities
● Interview parents about their understanding of the idea of 'costs' and 'benefits' in terms of decisions about a healthy lifestyle.
● Ask a guest speaker to talk to the children about how they have dedicated themselves to a particular 'healthy lifestyle' for sport or other reasons. Ask them to explain their idea of 'costs' and 'benefits'.

1 hour 30 mins What reasons are there for helping others?

Learning objectives
● Appreciate that some people relate 'healthy living' to helping others.
● Understand that costs and benefits can be related to voluntary work.

Lesson organisation
Introductory focus to the lesson and initial teacher-led discussion; paired activity; group activity; plenary.

Vocabulary
voluntary
benefit
value
empathy
community
reciprocal
worth
judgement

What you need and preparation
Make a collection of brochures and leaflets that illustrate voluntary schemes and projects in the community. You will also need newspaper articles that report local schemes and activities related to people working together. Provide a good supply of writing and drawing materials and make sure that you have access to a tape recorder and/or a video recorder.

What to do
20 mins **Introduction**
Introduce the idea that many people get a type of exercise that helps to improve their health and well-being by devoting their time to helping other people or contributing in some way to the community. Give the children some examples – you may have parents who help in school or you may know people who give up their time to record talking books for the blind or take disadvantaged children on outings. All these kinds of activities show examples of people who devote their energies, as well as their time, to helping other people. Encourage the children to think of any other cases they have heard of where similar contributions have been made by people to local projects.

Put the children into pairs and give each pair one of the leaflets or brochures that describe local voluntary projects. Ask them to rethink the format and content of the brochure so that it is not targeted at the people who need help but at those who might offer it. It should suggest that by contributing to these projects, people could improve their own health, lifestyle and well-being and, at the same time, benefit others. Remind them to use pictures as well as words.

After this first stage, ask the pairs to join with others to compare their work. Tell them to record the arguments they have used and decide which they think are the most convincing. If necessary, add a few prompts and additional ideas of your own, such as: *Working with people less fortunate than myself raises my own self-esteem but also makes me more sensitive to other people's needs. It makes me less selfish and less inward-looking.* Tell the children that

people say that giving their time and energies to others who are less fortunate than themselves makes them readdress problems that they have. It helps them to put things in perspective. Re-emphasise the point that this all contributes to producing a 'healthier' person – someone who is more aware, more sensitive and more sympathetic to other people's needs.

Invite the children to consider which of the projects represented would best show how this type of activity can improve the individual contributor's lifestyle. Tell them that their choice is going to be the basis for the next task. Some of the children may have done voluntary work themselves and could talk about how they feel they benefited.

1 hour Development

Organise the children into groups and explain that they are to create a radio or television advertisement to promote the idea that working for a voluntary project in the community can improve one's own health and lifestyle. This should be based on the project they have chosen earlier.

Ask the groups to allocate tasks to individual members – who will write the script, who will record it, who will shoot the video. They should also decide which of them will speak or act the parts. Encourage them to discuss their ideas with other adults and make any changes.

Once completed, they should show the finished 'product' to other children and adults, including parents, to get feedback on their advertisement.

10 mins Plenary

Discuss with the children the messages that they were trying to convey in their advertisements. Ask them to comment on one another's work and encourage them to ask each other for reasons and justifications. Do they think that their advertisement would attract people's attention, make them think and convince them to do something? Ask them to report what other children and adults felt about their work.

Suggest that they could compare their advertisement with one produced professionally and assess the differences.

Differentiation

The less able children will need help to use the brochures and leaflets effectively. Suggest phrases that they could use in the redesign of the brochure. More able children can use imagery to create the same impression.

Less able children will also require help with making the video, particularly with writing the script. Provide a structure within which they can write. More able children will be able to take on most elements of the task on their own.

Assessing learning outcomes

Are the children able to appreciate the idea of people benefiting personally from helping others? Can they put themselves 'in someone else's shoes' and represent their feelings and ideas? Do the children organise themselves effectively to produce their advertisement? Are they able to assess their advertisement objectively in relation to a 'professional' product?

ICT opportunities
Use the computer to produce graphics for both the redesigned brochure and the advertisement.

Follow-up activity
Invite a representative from a local community group to view the advertisements and provide some feedback and opinions on how effective it would be in persuading people to contribute.

Building healthy environments

This chapter adopts a broad interpretation of the term 'environment', recognising that we all function and participate in several 'environments'. It encompasses the physical and social environs in which the children are growing up and tackles the important interactions between the physical and human dimensions.

The activities in the chapter aim to develop the children's understanding and appreciation of a range of subjects and issues related to their environments. It is recognised that children of this age will be influenced by, and experience the pressures of, various aspects of those environments in which they live. It is also understood that the children themselves will have a part to play in shaping certain aspects of those environments, whether at home, at school, or, in the case of the older age range, the wider community.

There are also activities in the chapter that seek to develop children's understanding of the term 'healthy'. Clearly, there is a physical dimension to the idea, particularly in relation to the natural world – our countryside and the habitats of plants and animals. There is, however, an extended dimension to the term with regard to the quality of the life within those physical environs – and this dimension concerns issues such as care and protection. Throughout the chapter, the overriding aim is to help children develop a sense of responsibility, ownership and commitment to both the physical and social dimensions of their environments.

The chapter begins by addressing the issue of what the children understand to be, or not to be, 'their' environments, and to what extent some of these environments are personal or shared. Sense of belonging is the first important step towards taking responsibility for one's environments. The emphasis is on understanding the importance of taking personal responsibility.

The chapter progresses to consider in detail the concept of choice. It explores the fact that we have choices to make and that the choices we make affect and impact on our physical and social environments – the places where we work, play, relax and keep private. It points towards the benefits of positive behaviour and attitudes.

The chapter concludes with an exploration of the idea of pollution – what it is, the various forms it takes and how it affects people's lives. It addresses the issue that everyone is responsible, in one form or another, for 'polluting' the environment – and that this relates to our lifestyle, personal choices and attitudes.

Your life – your choice

This unit recognises that children's growing independence carries with it a number of important and interrelated considerations in terms of the 'environment' in which they are growing up.

Firstly, the children need to develop an understanding and appreciation of what constitutes their environment. This will obviously relate to the natural environment, the physical landscape, and extend to all forms of life that share it. However, there is a wider concept of environment that the unit explores, one that takes in the more personal and individual environment – areas where we work, play, seek solitude, relax and store possessions. The children are encouraged to think of these areas as 'their environment' and apply to them the basic principles of care, protection and responsibility.

As part of the consideration of what 'environment' is, the unit also examines the range of options and choices open to children in relation to their environments. As their options grow, so does their responsibility for the decisions they make. The children are introduced to the range of choices they may face, but are also encouraged to assess the importance of those choices. They are taught to appreciate that everyone, at some time in their life, has critical choices to make, and that those relating to our environment can be as critical as any others. The term 'health' has been explored in previous chapters, but here it is applied to the concept of the environment.

The second, and equally important, consideration of this unit is the development of critical skills such as analysis, evaluation and decision-making. The children are asked to look at their own community and assess its 'health', then find evidence for a presentation on the state of its 'fitness'. In another part of the unit the children make a series of decisions about part of their environment, choices related to its condition, its improvement and how these might be measured.

The third and final consideration of this unit is the exploration and development of attitudes and values. The children are asked to examine their own attitudes and are shown that these are very important ingredients of their character. They are asked to consider the notions of responsibility and ownership and the implications behind those terms. They will be introduced to vocabulary and concepts such as empathy and loyalty and be given opportunities to discuss a personal response to them.

The teacher's role is to act as a guide and facilitator, both of resources and ideas. Managing the learning process will involve orchestrating and encouraging the children's discussion, presentations, group work and assessment.

UNIT: Your life – your choice

Enquiry questions	Learning objectives	Teaching activities	Further teaching activities	Learning outcomes	Cross-curricular links
What do we understand by the term 'environment'? How does the quality of the environment directly affect people's lives?	• Understand that the term 'environment' has a number of meanings and applications. • Appreciate that the 'environment' is often a shared place.	Examine the wider concept of 'environment' and record feeling on this.	• Write a set of rules relating to 'My environment'. • Write about the environment from the perspective of another creature, or an object, whose habitat is threatened.	*Children:* • apply the concept of 'environment' to a range of contexts at a logical level • identify with different 'environments' in terms of their own values and responses • provide reasons for their ideas and opinions	Science: taking action to preserve the environment.
Do we affect our environment? How does the way people choose to behave affect how other people live their lives?	• Understand that everyone has choices about how they treat the environment. • Raise awareness of opportunities for choice in relation to the environment. • Appreciate that these choices may affect the lives of many people other than yourself.	Investigate people's attitudes to the environment, and the actions that could be taken to improve these. Make choices on the appropriate action for particular situations.	• Produce a poem or a jingle about 'choosing' - expressing positive feelings towards care of the environment. • Create a 'choice of the week' or 'choice of the month' award in the class or school which recognises individual children's positive choices related to their environment.	• appreciate the conscious or unconscious 'decision-making' distinction • provide reasons for people's conscious or unconscious behaviour distinguish between non-critical and critical choices	English: completing statement cards orally.
How can the term 'healthy' be applied to a community? How can remedies for a community be found?	• Understand that there are different interpretations of the word 'healthy'. • Appreciate that the term 'healthy' can be applied to a variety of contexts.	Consider the term 'health' as applied to a range of concepts. Identify 'healthy' and 'unhealthy' aspects of a selection of pictures.	• Extend the application of the terms 'healthy' and 'unhealthy' to the nation as a whole, giving examples from both categories. • Write from the perspective of someone coming to Earth and seeing examples of certain 'unhealthy behaviour'. How would they report this back to their fellow aliens?	• identify the factors involved in healthy and unhealthy environments • think in terms of 'remedies' for the unhealthy aspects of the environments	Health education: defining terms and ideas. English: writing labels for pictures.
How healthy is our environment? What evidence exists to indicate the healthy or unhealthy condition of the community?	• Appreciate that there are a number of perspectives to be considered in assessing health. • Understand that opinions differ on the definitions and assessment of what is healthy.	Plan and present a 'health check' of the places, organisations and people in their environment.	• Design a poster for display throughout the community that describes and explains to the public what they are trying to achieve. • Design a checklist and a set of criteria for a group of children to use in five years' time to check if things have improved in the community.	• develop an inclusive plan for the community 'health check' • incorporate the concept of 'community' and the concept of 'health' into their planning • work well together prepare a coherent and intelligible plan	Science or Geography: carrying out fieldwork. English: presenting results of the fieldwork.
Can we improve our environment? How can new developments within a community make a difference to its 'health'? How can individuals be encouraged to take more responsibility for their own community's health?	• Understand that actions to improve one's environment, however small, make a difference. • Appreciate that individuals have to take some responsibility for their own environment.	Identify an area that requires improvement and outline what needs to be done.	• Draft a proposal to apply for Lottery funding for their project. This should explain their aims and what they hope the project will achieve. • The children could plan a public launch of the project to gain local interest and support of it. They could plan the different elements of the launch in order to gain maximum publicity.	• apply their knowledge and skills to identifying an area, defining the problem and outlining their aims • achieve a reasonable level of agreement and conclusion on each stage of the task • resolve conflicts and differences of opinion satisfactorily • maintain a level of cohesion in working as a group • express opinions and assess the quality of their achievement.	English: writing a description of their proposed changes. Art and Design: producing drawings and pictures to go with their written descriptions.

1 hour What do we understand by the term 'environment'?

What you need and preparation

Collect sets of photographs or pictures of everyday scenes and stick these onto cards. These could include a house, a street, a school, a classroom, countryside and a town centre. You might also have pictures of a bus, train, car, shop, cinema or park. You will need enough to have at least one for each child.

Make, and enlarge, one copy each of photocopiable pages 125 and 126 and make a copy of photocopiable pages 127 and 128 for each child. You will also need writing and drawing materials.

What to do

15 mins Introduction

Introduce the term 'environment' and ask the children to suggest other words that explain it, or mean the same thing. They may suggest general terms like *area*, *place* and *our surroundings*. If they offer more specific examples, such as: *My room is my environment* then ask them why. Reasons could include, *I work there*, *I relax there*, *I keep things that belong to me there*.

Extend the idea of 'environment', moving from home, to street, then village, town or city, and to specific places, such as the park or swimming pool. Ask: *Is this your environment?* Explore the responses of the children to see if they feel as strongly about the 'extended' environment. Give each child a copy of photocopiable page 127 and ask them to illustrate their feelings. Some children may not see some sectors as 'their' environment at all; others will say it's a 'shared environment'. Examine the reasoning behind both of these perspectives.

Conclude this initial discussion with the following question: *Is the environment just a physical place?* This should stimulate the children to consider people and other living things as a part of the discussion.

30 mins Development

Model the activity that the children will undertake in groups by displaying the enlarged copies of photocopiable pages 125 and 126. Initiate a discussion, asking the children to express opinions on the two different environments. Ask: *Are these environments we care about and, if so, what measures do we need to take to look after them?*

Divide the class into groups of three and provide each group with a set of three photographs or pictures and the recording sheets (photocopiable page 128). Explain to the children that their task is to study their small pictures and make an assessment statement on each one on one of the recording sheets. Reaching agreement on the statements should involve discussion within the small group and an exchange of opinions that the children should record.

After a period of about ten minutes, pair the groups up and ask them to compare their conclusions. If time allows, invite each new group of six to draw a picture of an environment for which they care a great deal.

Conclude this part of the session with a whole-class discussion of the question: *Why do we seem to care more for some environments than for others?*

15 mins Plenary

Suggest that when people speak of 'their environment', they often have different ideas in mind. Ask the children: *How far does the idea of 'my environment' extend? Do you think your idea of 'my environment' may change, depending on your age, interests and knowledge?* Encourage them to ask people at home, including a grandparent, what they consider to be their

Learning objectives
● Understand that the term 'environment' has a number of meanings and applications.
● Appreciate that the 'environment' is often a shared place.

Lesson organisation
Initial teacher-led introduction and stimulus activity; group activity; whole-class discussion; plenary.

Vocabulary
environment
protect
maintain
sustain
responsibility
surroundings
global
community

ICT opportunities
Use the computer to add to the children's examples of 'my environment' and to produce their 'feelings map' (photocopiable page 127).

'environment'. Discuss how people who live in certain areas, and therefore consider that area 'their environment', often show concern about activities that may affect their lives. For example, people who live in the countryside may show concern at the possibility of a ban on hunting or about policies that might lead to the closure of rural shops or post offices.

If time allows, and there are children keen to pursue it, discuss concepts of 'my environment' that encompass a wider world view. Some children may be aware of, and concerned about, issues such as global warming or atmospheric pollution, but others may not. Examine these differing perspectives.

Differentiation

The less able children should still respond to the picture cards, though you may need to give them environments that will be more familiar to them. Offer help with the recording process, particularly if differences of opinion need to be represented.

More able children could illustrate one of the 'global' environmental issues as a basis for class discussion.

Assessing learning outcomes

Can the children apply the concept of 'environment' to a range of contexts at a logical level? Do they identify with different 'environments' in terms of their own values and responses? To what extent do the children view the environment as not 'theirs' at all? How well are they able to provide reasons for their ideas and opinions?

> **Follow-up activity**
> Prepare a very brief questionnaire or interview framework with the title 'My environment – my priorities'. Ask the children to work on suitable questions (probably no more than four) that will provide an insight into what others consider to be 'their environment'. Each child could then interview one, or more, adults.

How do we affect our environment?

(1 hour)

> **Learning objectives**
> ● Understand that everyone has choices about how they treat the environment.
> ● Raise awareness of opportunities for choice in relationship to the environment.
> ● Appreciate that these choices may affect the lives of many people other than yourself.

What you need and preparation

Prepare a series of 'choice' cards from photocopiable page 130. Make a set for each group. These could be laminated to give them extra protection. Find a few local newspaper articles that deal with the issue of caring for the environment. Make a copy of photocopiable page 129 for each child. Provide writing and drawing materials.

What to do

Introduction
(25 mins)

Introduce the idea that, either consciously or unconsciously, we all make choices about how we treat our environment. Some of us drop litter occasionally, or we may leave a room untidy or make unnecessary noise that disturbs other people. Ask the children to think of other examples, stimulated by questions such as: *What kinds of behaviour show a lack of consideration for the environment? What types of behaviour with regard to the environment upset you?*

Use articles from local newspapers to illustrate people's lack of care for their surroundings – both physical and human. Ask the children: *Why do you think people choose to behave in this way? Do they deliberately choose to do these things or do they do them without thinking?* Give each child a copy of photocopiable page 129 and ask them to complete the storyboard.

Pursue the idea of choice by suggesting that we are often faced with a range of choices relating to our environment. List the phrases from photocopiable page 130 (choice cards) on the board and use these to illustrate the type of choices that could be made (to do something or not to do something; to stop doing something or not stop doing something; to persuade

Your life - your
choice

others to your point of view or to leave it up to them). Then ask for a few examples of behaviour that complete the statements on the cards, discussing what opportunities they raise for choice. This will be expanded in 'Development'. Discuss the idea of conscious and unconscious choice and what factors might determine conscious and unconscious choices.. Suggest, for example, that people may consciously choose to use the recycling facilities in their town (perhaps because they have been actively persuaded that they will benefit from the extra effort involved), while people putting litter in a waste paper basket probably do it unconsciously (because it usually requires minimum effort and is something they have been taught to do from early on). Encourage the children to respond to this by giving examples from their own experiences.

20 mins Development

Divide the class into groups and give each a set of the 'choice' cards on photocopiable page 130. Ask the groups to place the cards face down on the table and then take turns to pick up a card. Tell them that each child must then make two personal statements in response to the phrase on the card that is chosen, such as: *I would not do anything about someone who I saw smoking in a non-smoking place or who I heard playing their car radio too loud;* or *I would do something about someone who I saw was letting their dog foul the pavement or who I saw damaging plants in the park.* The idea behind the activity is twofold: to try to broaden children's thinking about the choices available to them; and to make them aware of the opportunities for responsible action their own concerns provide. After each child has made his or her responses, any member of the group can comment, challenge or offer an alternative choice. One child in each group should act as scribe and record at least two important statements or ideas from the group's discussions. The next child then picks up a card.

At the end of the group task session, ask the scribe to share the important statements or ideas with the rest of the class. They should give a specific reason as to why they chose to report those statements. Invite the other members of the group to comment too and encourage questions from others in the class to clarify what was meant.

15 mins Plenary

Point out that some choices we have to make are reasonably easy – what to eat for breakfast or what to wear to a party. Although we may sometimes spend a lot of time making these choices (particularly the latter!), they are not critical choices on which a great deal depends. Ask the children if they can think of other examples.

Lesson organisation
Initial teacher introduction and stimulus activity; group activity and reporting of ideas; whole-class discussion; plenary.

Vocabulary
opportunities
priorities
preferences
values
worth

ICT opportunities
Produce the storyboard and storyline on the computer.

Follow-up activity
Check the local press or the news for examples of incidents where critical choices or decisions have been made that affect other people's lives or the environment. The children should record how they would have felt if they had been asked to make that choice.

Go on to say that other choices we make are more critical because they may have a huge effect on our lives, and perhaps the lives of others. Illustrate this in relation to the environment, by giving the example of a group of children who deliberately choose to vandalise a play area in their neighbourhood. Compare this with a group of children who devote some of their spare time to doing chores and odd jobs for the elderly people in their street.

Return to the work the children did in 'Development' and determine whether it indicates opportunities for them, either as individuals or as a class, to choose to do something that will benefit their school environment – for example: to provide more receptacles for litter and posters to encourage using them; to suggest practical and achievable ways to improve the appearance of their classroom; to set up a system for collecting items that can be reused or recycled (paper, plastic containers and so on).

Differentiation
Offer the less able children help in the form of visual stimulus with the 'choice' cards and support their reporting process by providing questions to which they just add a short phrase.

The more able children could design some more choice statements to develop the idea.

Assessing learning outcomes
Can the children appreciate the conscious or unconscious 'decision-making' distinction? Can they provide reasons for people's conscious or unconscious behaviour? Can the children distinguish between non-critical and critical choices? Can they apply them to their own experiences? Do they appreciate that a choice they make may have implications for others? Can the children identify opportunities for choice in their environments?

(1 hour) How can the term 'healthy' be applied to our community?

Learning objectives
● Understand that there are different interpretations of the word 'healthy'.
● Appreciate that the term 'healthy' can be applied to a variety of contexts.

Lesson organisation
Introductory teacher-led focus and initial stimulus activity; group activity; presentation and of outcomes; whole-class discussion.

What you need and preparation
Make sets of pictures of everyday places from photocopiable page 131. You will need several sets. Prepare cards for the children to use as labels and writing and drawing materials. You will also need access a board or flipchart.

What to do
(10 mins) Introduction
Introduce the term 'healthy' to the class and ask them to think of other words that they associate with it. They may suggest: *body, environment, family* or *church*. Write these words on the board to remind the children.

Now ask them to think of phrases that help to explain the word 'healthy' more precisely. Expect suggestions such as: *in good shape, working well*, and *fit*. Write these phrases on the board too as a reminder.

Ask the children if 'unhealthy' means simply the opposite of healthy. *Does it mean 'unfit' or can we use other words like 'unpleasant', 'nasty', 'unsafe' or 'risky'?* This line of questioning is intended to explore the children's values, as well as their linguistic skills.

(40 mins) Development
Divide the class into groups and give each group a set of photographs or pictures and some small cards on which to write labels.

Explain that their task is to look at each picture and think about all the reasons why that object or setting could be described as 'healthy' or 'unhealthy'. Suggest, for example, that they

might say for 'house': *The house is healthy because the people who live there take regular exercise and eat a balanced diet.* Encourage the children to think in as wide a sense as possible about the concept of the 'healthy house', asking: *What other sense of 'healthy' can we apply to the house?* As an example suggest to them that the house might be considered 'healthy' because it lets in a lot of sunlight.

Then ask: *So why could the house be described as 'unhealthy'?* By this time the children should catch on to the concept, and give answers such as: *There is a person who lives there who smokes. There is no insulation in the loft. The woodwork around the window frames is rotten.* Write their thoughts down on one of the labels, using the headings 'Healthy' and 'Unhealthy'. Ask the groups to complete a similar label for each picture.

When the exercise is concluded, select a child from each group to present the information on one of their labels. Try to cover all the pictures on the photocopiable sheet. Ask the children to look for similarities in the descriptors of what is 'healthy' and 'unhealthy' across the different examples. Put these suggestions on the board for the plenary session.

(10 mins) Plenary

Focus on the descriptors for what is 'unhealthy'. These may well encompass wider implications such as atmospheric pollution, noise pollution, poorly designed buildings or lack of waste management. Talk to the children about remedies. Explain that if something is unhealthy, people usually ask: *What is the remedy?* Ask the children to produce a prescription listing some possible remedies for those things that they described as 'unhealthy'.

Differentiation

The less able children may need some initial word clues added to the set of pictures. Alternatively, give them a set of words and ask for these to be placed on the appropriate picture – references to 'healthy' food and exercise might go with the house, for example.

More able children could be asked in the plenary to prescribe a selection of remedies, rather than just one for the specific problem.

Assessing learning outcomes

Are the children able to identify the factors involved in healthy and unhealthy environments? Are they generally more positive or negative in their labelling of environments? Are they able to think in terms of 'remedies' for the unhealthy aspects of the environments?

Vocabulary
beneficial
supportive
empathy
understanding
encouraging
unhealthy
organisation
community

ICT opportunities
Word-process a remedy, in the form of a prescription, for one of the unhealthy conditions.

Follow-up activity
Design an illustrated and annotated poster for one of the places illustrated on the photocopiable sheet to show the relevant concepts of healthy and unhealthy.

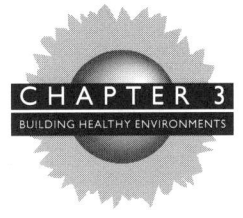

Your life – your
choice

1 hour How healthy is our community?

**Learning
objectives**
● Appreciate that
there are a number
of perspectives to
be considered in
assessing health.
● Understand that
opinions differ on
the definitions and
assessment of what
is healthy.

**Lesson
organisation**
Introductory
teacher-led focus
and initial stimulus
activity; group
activity then
presentation and
publishing of
outcomes; whole-
class discussion.

Vocabulary
symptom
remedy

What you need and preparation

Prepare and display a large map of your local area on which the children can mark places, organisations and people who are to be given the health check. Enlarge a copy of photocopiable page 132 to use as stimulus in the 'Introduction'. Make a list of community organisations on the board or flipchart. Collect some photographs of particular places within the area that might help to focus the thoughts of the less able children on aspects of the topic.

What to do

20 mins Introduction

Organise the children into groups and explain that the activity is a planning exercise. They are going to plan a 'health check' of their environment, using the factors and criteria that they identified in the previous activity. The 'health check' is a fact-finding exercise based on the community from which they will choose one area to develop in the next activity, 'Your environment – your choice'). Emphasise that, if time permits, they will be carrying out the plan they make later. (Carrying out their plans might be accommodated as part of field work in science or geography.)

Remind the children of the various definitions of the term 'environment' that they have already discussed in other lessons. It can include places, organisations, areas and people. They must include all of these when planning their survey of the area. Show them that they will have a map and photographs to help them think about their area and a list of local organisations. Remind them too of the meaning of 'health' that has been discussed.

Suggest that the children need to consider the following for their health check:
● The areas, organisations and individuals they wish to include. Show them photocopiable page 132 as a prompt of the things they should try to check.
● Who they would talk to – they should think of the 'type' of person they would find within each place or organisation they have chosen.
● What they would ask them – what it is like to be working, living or playing there.
● What other evidence they should collect – sounds, photographs, or people's opinions.
● When would be a good time to carry out their health check.

Help the groups to divide the tasks listed above among their members and allocate responsibilities for recording and writing conclusions. Give them a timeframe in which to work, such as 15 minutes to brainstorm questions and then report to the rest of their group on what they have decided.

**ICT
opportunities**
The plan,
questionnaire and
interview schedule
can all be
produced on the
computer.

 Development

The children will need more than one 30-minute session to plan the health check so you will need to adapt the lesson to suit the time you have available.

Each time they work on this task bring the groups together at the end of the session to report on the progress they have made and give the other groups the chance to add their suggestions. Ask each group to appoint someone to record what they have achieved and publish this progress report on a 'bulletin board' at intervals.

Keep the large map of the area on the wall throughout to act as a reminder, and as a means of reporting what aspects of the 'community' have been covered.

Plenary

Ask the children to present their health check plan as a group. They should give the reasons for their decisions and explain their strategy.

During the plenary you should also examine the children's views on how well the groups worked together and how easily they agreed on ways to fulfil the task.

Differentiation

Help the less able children with planning this exercise. They might concentrate on just one aspect, perhaps making a list of the people and organisations to whom they should send the health check. Provide some headings for their questionnaire or interview schedule, then leave them to complete it.

Ask more able children to think of follow-up questions to the basic interviews.

Assessing learning outcomes

Are the children able to develop an inclusive plan for the community 'health check'? Can they incorporate the concept of 'community' and the concept of 'health' into their planning? Do the children work well together? Is their plan coherent and intelligible to other groups in the class?

> **Follow-up activity**
> Try to schedule time for actually carrying out the health check either as additional PSHE time or as part of time in another curriculum area such as science or geography. This will obviously require planning for safety and adult supervision. Alternatively, carry out a limited version of the health check by asking children to select particular people to meet or to send questionnaires.

Can we improve our environment?

What you need and preparation

You will need one or more of the following maps – an outline plan of the school, a map of the local area, a plan of your local village or town. Collect some photographs of places within the selected sites. Make a copy of photocopiable page 133 for each group.

What to do

15 mins Introduction

Divide the class into groups and take them through the elements of the task. Explain that the first task is for each group to identify an environment within the area – this may be part of the school, part of the local village or town, or part of the area surrounding the school or town. It might be a building or an existing amenity which, in the opinion of the group, needs some improvement. Suggest that each group should choose this environment by taking an imaginary walk around the area, then focusing on a particular place. Ask each child to suggest one potential environment. The group should then discuss these suggestions and make a choice.

The second task is for the group to describe and define what aspect of their chosen environment needs to be improved. This will require an explanation and some evidence to support their case. If possible it should include visual evidence, such as a photograph or drawing.

> **Learning objectives**
> ● Understand that actions to improve one's environment, however small, make a difference.
> ● Appreciate that individuals have to take some responsibility for their own environment.

Your life – your choice

Lesson organisation
Teacher-led introductory focus and initial stimulus activity; group activity then reporting and publishing of outcomes; whole-class discussion, plenary.

Vocabulary
responsibility
ownership
commitment
initiative
priority
input
change
effectiveness

The children should also indicate the possible level of support for their case from other people.

The third task is for the group to define their aims for the 'environment'. These should be expressed as intentions and should be supported with reasons.

30 mins **Development**
The groups will need more than one 30-minute session to complete all aspects of the 'strategy' stage. Time will determine how far the children can develop their strategy.

Ask the groups to write a description of their proposed changes and an outline of what they believe is needed to achieve these changes. Encourage them to support the written description with drawings and diagrams. If time permits, some members of the group could visit the 'environment' to collect other on-site evidence to support their written and visual descriptions.

Finally, the children should consider how they would measure the success of the improvements they are proposing and how these might make an impact on any people who are in contact with the area.

Give each group a copy of photocopiable page 133 and ask them to complete it as they make their decisions.

ICT opportunities
All the proposed plans and diagrams could be developed on the computer using a graphics package.

Follow-up activity
Ask the children to produce their proposed changes as a formal proposal and find someone to read and comment on these, perhaps a local councillor or the headteacher. These people might also be prepared to speak to the children about their ideas.

15 mins **Plenary**
Ask the groups to discuss why they chose particular areas and gauge the level of agreement amongst them. Consider too the extent to which the problems of the particular 'environment' have been defined and the groups' estimation of the scale of the problem.

Differentiation
The less able children may need help to identify an area. Encourage them to consider the school and its grounds, as these are 'closer to home'. They may also need to be provided with some key questions in order to define the problem of the 'environment'. Defining aims could be done visually by some children.

Encourage more able children to draw up a longer-term plan for their chosen place, perhaps over three years.

Assessing learning outcomes
Can the children apply their knowledge and skills to identifying an area, defining the problem and outlining their aims? Are the children able to achieve a reasonable level of agreement and conclusions on each stage of the task? Can they resolve conflicts and differences of opinion satisfactorily? Can the groups maintain a level of cohesion when working together? Are the children able to express opinions and assess the quality of their achievement?

Pollution – who's to blame?

This unit focuses on developing the concept of 'pollution' across a range of contexts. The children will probably be familiar with some of the areas to which the term is applied – land, water, air and atmosphere – but this unit helps them to understand that pollution can be applied to other contexts and can take on a range of other forms.

Responsibility for pollution is often laid at the door of industry and commerce – organisations engaged in the manufacture of potentially harmful substances or using manufacturing processes that create waste. One of the purposes of this unit is to extend the children's understanding of the nature of society's responsibility as a whole for the quality of its environment. It explains that society places demands on its 'providers' for products that are thought to improve the quality of life, and that these have a 'cost' in terms of the quality of the environment. This idea can be developed to include discussion of the less-frequently discussed environmental consequences, such as the impact of stressful working environments on people's health.

The unit also considers pollution in the context of the physical environment. Through practical activities and tasks, the children are invited to examine selected aspects of the term 'pollution' as they apply to land, air and water. Again, emphasis is placed on the way in which personal choice and subsequent human behaviour cause pollution. Strictly speaking, cars, lorries and buses are not the polluters, rather it is the people who demand these and then behave irresponsibly once they have them.

The unit endeavours to help children understand and appreciate the issues from a variety of standpoints. In some activities they are expected to make a personal response, and express their own views, opinions, and interests. In other parts of the unit, they are encouraged to view the issues from other people's perspectives and assess how personal interest can play a part in choices. Finally, the unit invites the children to think about how people's attitudes and behaviour can be changed (or not) and the influences that might be used to try to achieve this change.

The teacher's role is to guide the children – identifying ideas for their consideration, offering alternative viewpoints and providing additional, relevant data. In order to manage the learning process it will be necessary to ensure that the children have adequate opportunities to express their viewpoints and that others respect them and are prepared to listen and tolerate their opinions.

Unit: Pollution – who's to blame?

Enquiry questions	Learning objectives	Teaching activities	Further teaching activities	Learning outcomes	Cross-curricular links
Who shares the responsibility for pollution in our society? What are the costs to our society of the various forms of pollution?	● Understand what pollution is, and the various forms it can take. ● Understand that everyone, to some extent, pollutes his or her own environment. ● Identify effective ways of persuading people to change their behaviour.	Develop a pollution quiz. Produce some anti-pollution literature.	● Set up a 'Pollution Watch', recording instances of pollution that they see or hear about in their area, and then record if anything is done about it. ● Design a 'costings chart' which graphically, through pictures, drawings and charts shows the cost of pollution to our society, in terms of health, work, animals and buildings.	*Children:* ● grasp that there is a very wide set of parameters for the word 'pollution' ● understand and accept that everyone, in some sense, is a polluter ● appreciate that everyone is affected by even the most minor acts of pollution ● formulate their message in the leaflet or poster in a way that illustrates that they understand the idea of persuasive language	Science: pollution in the environment. Art and Design: producing anti-pollution posters. English: using persuasive language.
What forms of pollution affect the land? How does land pollution affect people and animals?	● Understand that land pollution is caused by the actions of individuals, as well as companies and governments. ● Appreciate that land pollution affects plants, animals and humans, as well as the land itself.	Discuss land pollution. Script and storyboard a film about land pollution for young children.	● Draw up a system of 'fines' for different activities that cause land pollution. ● Carry out a 'waste survey' based on what the children and their families throw away each week.	● understand the wider concept of pollution and the many forms that it can take ● respond to the idea of the serious consequences that can arise from these irresponsible acts ● respond to experiences or instances of pollution in their own area ● script and storyboard the incident ● relate to the idea of the 'throwaway society' from their own experiences	Science: preserving the land. English: writing scripts. English/Art and Design: creating storyboards.
What forms of air pollution affect the quality of our lives? How does the lifestyle people lead affect the quality of the environment?	● Appreciate that air pollution is caused by a number of personal and public actions. ● Understand that air pollution affects people in many different ways.	Identify types of air pollution and how they are caused. Design a family board game on the theme of pollution. Discuss ways of changing people's behaviour.	● Hold a meeting between Marlton Council and some of those protesting against their anti-air-pollution campaign. ● Write a letter to the council from someone protesting against one aspect of their campaign.	● appreciate the various ways in which our atmosphere is polluted ● understand that public demand is, in many ways, as much responsible for pollution as any other organisation ● appreciate the problem of trying to persuade people to change their behaviour patterns	Science: clean air and atmosphere.
What are the major sources of water pollution? What can individuals do to reduce the risk of pollution in their community?	● Understand that pollution affects the quality of our water and endangers health. ● Appreciate that the causes of pollution are sometimes difficult to trace	Talk about ways in which water pollution occurs. Debate an instance of water pollution from the standpoints of various interested parties.	● Produce a leaflet for the public which explains one aspect of water pollution and suggests ways of preventing it happening in rivers, streams or canals. ● Write a letter to the local council about an incident of water pollution.	● represent other people's points of view ● respond to differing points of view and conflicting evidence ● look for imaginative explanations for the pollution ● respond to the idea of punishment for people or organisations found responsible for pollution	Science: clean water. English: speaking and listening – debating a pollution issue.
Pollution – a worldwide problem? What kinds of measures are being taken to improve matters?	● Appreciate that pollution is a problem that affects countries all over the world. ● Understand that governments set targets to try to improve environmental pollution.	Discuss air pollution across the world and the action taken by governments to combat it. Create a world pollution map.	● Plan a Pupil Action Against Pollution (PAAP) campaign enlisting the support of children all over the world. How would you get children interested? ● Write a letter to a local MP asking what current action the government is taking on pollution and what it is doing on a global scale to improve the quality of people's lives.	● appreciate how one country's individual and domestic activities can affect another ● appreciate that the problems of pollution are sufficiently serious to warrant greater government action.	Geography: pollution as a worldwide concern. Science: clean air.

(1 hour) Who shares the responsibility for pollution in our society?

What you need and preparation

Make a collection of pictures that illustrate the wider concept of pollution. These might include: a factory chimney, roads with congested traffic, a polluted river showing dead fish. Pictures that introduce the idea of noise and visual pollution could also be valuable: large billboards or posters on walls, loud machinery or music. Expand the idea further with a picture of an untidy bedroom or school cloakroom. Make a copy of photocopiable page 134 for each group. Provide writing and drawing materials for making posters.

What to do

(15 mins) Introduction

Suggest that, when the word 'pollution' is introduced, there is a tendency to think of the obvious sources. Factories, cars and buses are usually considered to cause environmental pollution, and this is generally thought of in terms of damage to plants and wildlife. Prove this point by playing a word association game with the children, asking them to suggest other words that they associate with pollution.

Develop the idea that pollution means anything that is introduced into our lives (or environment) that is potentially harmful to us. Define the word 'harm', if necessary. Then explore the idea of 'harm', starting with the harm that can be caused to our physical health by dangerous substances. Talk to the children about some examples of harmful substances. Move on to consider a wider definition of 'harm' that includes our mental or emotional state – what harm, in additional to physical harm to our ears, might be done by continuous noise – this could be from a factory, a road, or loud music. Ask the children to think of some more examples.

Organise the children into groups and give each group a copy of photocopiable page 134. Explain that they are to think up some more pollution questions and add them to the photocopiable sheet. Once each group has ten questions they should challenge another group to see how well they score.

(35 mins) Development

Divide the class into groups and share out the pictures of different forms of pollution. Ask them to consider how they as individuals might be contributing to the kinds of pollution depicted. Explain that each group is to produce a leaflet or poster for the theme 'Pollution – what do you mean… me?' It should illustrate their perceptions of themselves as polluters and include some suggestions of things that they might do to combat pollution. The idea is that the leaflet or poster should identify what causes pollution, but also have a positive message about what can be done to remedy it.

Suggest to the children that they begin by writing some text and drawing pictures to illustrate their ideas. Encourage them to place the artwork around the text, and to use banner headlines, facts and figures and catchy phrases, such as *No to noise*, *Polluters – push off*, *Pollution – not a problem*, *Save it* or *Recycle it*.

Display the completed leaflets and posters and invite comments and opinions from other groups in the class.

Learning objectives
● Understand what pollution is and the various forms it can take.
● Understand that everyone, to some extent, pollutes his or her own environment.
● Identify effective ways of persuading people to change their behaviour.

Lesson organisation
Initial teacher-led discussion and stimulus activity; group activity then presentation and publishing of work; group discussion; plenary.

Vocabulary
pollution
responsibility
consequences

CHAPTER 3
BUILDING HEALTHY ENVIRONMENTS

Pollution –
who's to
blame?

10 mins Plenary
Discuss with the children the problem of trying to get a message across to an audience. Ask them: *Do you think you have managed to get your message across?*

Talk about the various ways of making an impact with a message – frightening people into action; showing them unpleasant images; making them feel guilty; pointing out the consequences of their behaviour; offering practical rather than negative information, and so on.

Ask the children to think about, and discuss, which methods influence them to change their behaviour. *What methods would not persuade you to change?*

Differentiation

The less able children will require practical examples, such as continuous unpleasant noise, to help them understand the wider concept of pollution. They will also need support to understand the wider definition of the term 'harm' beyond its usual physical meaning. Drawing on some personal experiences may help this process.

More able children are more likely to be able see themselves as participants in global pollution issues, not necessarily as 'first-hand' polluters, but as 'consumers' who demand products or processes that involve pollution. Encourage them to think of chains of cause and effect.

Assessing learning outcomes

Can the children grasp that there is a very wide set of parameters for the word 'pollution'? Are they able to understand and accept that everyone, in some sense, is a polluter? Are they able to appreciate that everyone is affected by even the most minor acts of pollution? Can they formulate the message in their leaflet or poster in a way that illustrates that they understand the idea of persuasive language?

ICT opportunities
Use a graphics package to develop the leaflets or posters.
Follow-up activity
Ask the children to consider other ways of getting the pollution message across to other audiences, such as an assembly presentation for the rest of the school, a short 'sound bite' for a local radio station, or a design for a website.

1 hour What forms of pollution affect the land?

What you need and preparation

Collect pictures or photographs that show forms of land pollution. The Environment Agency (your local division should be listed in Yellow Pages) has education officers in all regions of the country who will be able to help provide this type of resource. Alternatively, the pictures on photocopiable page 135 could be used for this. The children will also need writing and drawing materials, including large sheets of paper suitable for storyboards.

What to do

15 mins Introduction
Tell the children that land pollution is quite a serious problem in Britain. It has been estimated that there could be as many as 20 000 sites in the country that are contaminated, and these add up to a very large area of land. Distribute copies of photocopiable page 135 or the pictures you collected and use them to discuss some of the issues.

Talk to the children about any experiences they may have of local pollution – they may offer instances of people dumping things in fields or at the side of the road, or leaving litter on beaches or in parks.

Discuss the idea that some people do these things without thinking and that they are unaware of the consequences, while other people deliberately dump things on the land to try to get rid of a problem. This could be members of the public, it could be companies, sometimes even farmers have been guilty of dumping contaminated items on the land. Explain that, in some cases, governments have been accused of polluting the environment and in these cases the

Learning objectives
● Understand that land pollution is caused by the actions of individuals as well as companies and governments.
● Appreciate that land pollution affects plants, animals and humans, as well as the land itself.

Lesson organisation
Teacher-led introductory focus to the lesson and stimulus activity; group activity then display of work; whole-class discussion.

consequences for large numbers of people and large areas of land are very serious, with risks also to wildlife, property, water and air.

Development

30 mins Divide the class into groups and explain that their task is to script and storyboard a short film about land pollution for young children. They should use a story format. Tell them that they can choose their own subject, but make a few suggestions such as: *someone abandons a broken-down car in a field*; *a farmer clears a wooded area to make a grazing field for cows*; *someone leaves all their camping rubbish on a beach* or *someone leaves bags of litter in a street*.

Tell them that they should begin by describing how the incident happened, showing the sequence of events and the people involved. They should then show the consequences of what happened for those people directly responsible and for anyone else who was directly or indirectly affected. One half of the group should produce the script, possibly using characters and a narrative, voice-over commentary, while the other half of the group should take responsibility for producing the storyboard.

Ask each group of children to describe their story and storyboard to another group in order to share their ideas before finalising their versions.

This part of the activity could well be linked to a literacy session focusing on writing playscripts.

Plenary

15 mins Discuss with the children the idea that everyone has some responsibility for polluting the land. *How can that statement be true?*

Talk with the children about the subject of waste. Ask them about their experiences of waste – do they realise that many of the goods we buy come in packages that end up as waste? Do they understand that managing the waste products that are produced is a problem? They may know ways of helping people to manage their own waste, such as bottle and paper banks.

Take a little time to explore the underlying causes of the 'waste' problem: *Do we live in a 'throwaway' society?*

Differentiation

The less able children will need help with the film script and storyboard. Provide them with headings under which they can write, or complete some parts of their storyboard for them and ask them to fill the gaps. Alternatively they could use the photographs or pictures as stimuli and use these to write their own story.

More able children could produce a full script and background sounds for their short film.

Assessing learning outcomes

Can the children understand the wider concept of pollution and the many forms that it can take? How do they respond to the idea of the serious consequences that can arise from these irresponsible acts? How do they feel about experiences or instances of pollution in their own area? How well do the children cope with scripting and storyboarding the incident? Can they relate to the idea of the 'throwaway society' from their own experiences?

ICT opportunities
Scripting and storyboarding the incident could be done on the computer.

Follow-up activity
Ask the children to look at the issue of waste in their home and find out what happens to paper, cardboard, bottles and garden rubbish. Investigate what your local council does to help residents sort out their waste.

① What forms of air pollution affect the quality of our lives?

**Learning
objectives**
● Appreciate that
air pollution is
caused by a variety
of personal and
public actions.
● Understand that
air pollution affects
people in many
different ways.

**Lesson
organisation**
Teacher-led
introductory focus
to the lesson and
stimulus activity;
group activity, then
reporting, review
and display of
work; group
discussion; plenary.

What you need and preparation
Make several sets of cards labelled with sources of pollution, such as car, lorry, bus, smokers, factory, fires, and so on. Provide large sheets of paper and drawing materials to make the snakes and ladders games. Make copies of photocopiable page 136.

What to do
15 mins **Introduction**
Distribute copies of photocopiable page 136. Read the newspaper extract with the children and use the text to promote discussion on air pollution – what it is and what forms it takes. Alternatively you could find some stories related to air pollution in the local or national press. Ask the children to identify the types of air pollution mentioned and discuss each of these in terms of everyday activities, particularly in relationship to your own environment.

Increasing road traffic is an obvious cause of air pollution. Traffic is responsible for over 80% of carbon monoxide emissions and this is one of the reasons why all governments have to plan transport policies and structures. They hope to remedy the situation by building ring roads, improving public transport and creating park and ride schemes.

Emissions from manufacturing and industrial processing also contribute significantly to air pollution, particularly in city environments. Discuss the fact that people's demands for a higher quality of life puts pressure on industry to produce new products and that power stations (which are responsible for 65% of sulphur dioxide emissions) have to generate more power to meet this public demand. You might mention that there is legislation relating to emissions and that laws on local emissions in the 1980s significantly reduced levels of pollution.

Now talk to the children about how pollution of the air may come from other everyday activities – for example, burning rubbish and smoky heating fuels; smoking cigars and cigarettes; using aerosols.

Discuss how people's attitudes affect the way that they behave. If people believe that they can do what they like with their own possessions, irrespective of the consequences, then they will see throwing them away, dumping or burning them, as options. Mention too that population growth contributes to air pollution.

35 mins **Development**
Divide the class up into small groups (about four) and set them the task of producing a family snakes and ladders game based on the theme of pollution. Tell them that they can make the game as complicated as they wish and that they can use all types of pollution; they need not restrict themselves to aspects of air pollution discussed in the 'Introduction'.

Suggest that they start by thinking about the design of the board. They will need negative statements for the snakes, such as: *garden fire produces complaints from neighbours*; and positive statements for the ladders, such as: *schoolchildren introduce paper-recycling scheme*.

Encourage them to think about the game being played by a family. Remind them that there should be positive and negative statements for different members of the family, both adults and children. They should also include additional bonus statements for particular family actions, such as using bottle banks or sorting rubbish for recycling.

Encourage them to play the game in outline, getting suggestions from other groups in order to improve their product.

Vocabulary
atmosphere
unpleasant
quality
emissions
ozone
pollutants
consumption

10 **Plenary**
mins

Introduce the subject of trying to persuade people to change the way they behave and discuss the various strategies employed by governments and other agencies to make people take more responsibility for their actions. Taxing car users for using their cars in inner cities and introducing road tolls are just two of many schemes proposed – discuss these from the point of view of a motorist.

Talk to the children about trying to control people's behaviour, by law if necessary, in order to ensure the quality of the environment. Ask if they think it is a good idea to limit the use of cars in towns, or pay people to reduce their waste products. Talk about what is done in school in terms of a 'clean air' policy and ask: *What would you do if you had the power to make changes?*

Differentiation

Help the less able children to design the snakes and ladders game. Provide some of the statements for the board or allow them to complete a partly-designed board. Less able children will also be able to pick ideas for their design from discussion with other groups.

More able children could introduce statements into the game that relate to other organisations, not just a family, such as a factory, or a shop.

Assessing learning outcomes

Can the children appreciate the various ways in which our atmosphere is polluted? Can they understand that public demand is, in many ways, as much responsible for pollution as any other organisation? Can they appreciate the problem of trying to persuade people to change their behaviour patterns? Can they see the role that the law might play in changing people's behaviour?

ICT opportunities
The snakes and ladders game could be designed and played on the computer.

Follow-up activities
● Look for articles in local or national newspapers or magazines that refer to air pollution problems. Ask the children to write their own thoughts and responses to the situations described.
● Use time in music or art to design and produce a 'clean air' jingle or poster.

1 **What are the major sources of water pollution?**
hour

What you need and preparation

Make set of cards (enough for one card for each group) with the following labels: *local councillor, farmer, fisherman, director of local upholstery business, warden of local park, owner of golf course, holidaymaker on caravan park, local resident.* Prepare and display an enlarged copy of the map on photocopiable page 137.

What to do

15 **Introduction**
mins

Introduce the subject of water pollution, explaining that rivers, streams, canals and ponds are just some of the areas that can be affected by pollution. There may be a local example (polluted or not) on which the children could be invited to comment.

Talk about the ways in which pollution could occur. Rivers could be polluted by a company discharging waste into them, by farmers putting chemicals on their land which then seep into the river, by holidaymakers in boats dumping rubbish into them and so on.

Point out that many people feel strongly about pollution and that, when the subject of damage to the environment is mentioned, many different interest groups are anxious to express their point of view. Often these viewpoints conflict.

30 **Development**
mins

Divide the class into groups. Give each group one card and tell them that they represent the person or organisation given on the card.

Learning objectives
● Understand that pollution affects the quality of our water and endangers health.
● Appreciate that the causes of pollution are sometimes difficult to trace.

Lesson organisation
Teacher-led introductory focus to the lesson and stimulus activity; group role-play then whole-class discussion.

Vocabulary
spillage
consumption
waste
responsibility
standards
quality

CHAPTER 3
BUILDING HEALTHY ENVIRONMENTS

Pollution –
who's to
blame?

Explain that all these people live in the same area. Indicate the map and explain that the river that runs through this area has been very badly polluted. The cause of this is not obvious, but there is plenty of evidence of the pollution, such as dead fish in the river, farm animals that have become sick, and damaged plant life.

Explain to the group that they have to think about the pollution to the river and describe how their person or organisation is affected by it. They should write down their 'case' and then present it to the rest of the class.

Bring the groups together to present and debate their cases. Then ask the children to look at the map through the eyes of their interested party and try to identify possible explanations for the pollution. If some of the groups are accused of being responsible, then they should defend themselves. The solution or answer may not be revealed, but it is the process of debating the issues that is important.

15 mins **Plenary**

Discuss the issue of water pollution by taking one of the explanations the children have suggested and considering its cause, and its consequences. Ask the children for their opinions. How would they deal with a serious incident of river pollution if they were an Environment Agency and discovered that someone was dumping waste into a local river? Encourage them to imagine a particular case.

Talk about people's behaviour in relation to water pollution: *Can their behaviour and attitudes be changed? Should punishments be imposed, and what would be appropriate?*

Differentiation

The less able children might need some help with taking on their roles and you may need to provide some clues to the ideas and opinions that a fisherman, for example, might take. They could also be given one or two possible reasons for the pollution or picture clues to which they add an explanation.

More able children could take on the role of Environment Agency representatives and investigate the explanations that the other groups offer for the pollution.

Assessing learning outcomes

How well do the children cope with representing other people's points of view? Can they respond to differing points of view and conflicting evidence? How imaginative are they in looking for explanations for the pollution? How do they respond to the idea of punishment for people or organisations found responsible for pollution?

ICT opportunities
Produce a newspaper report of the pollution incident with drawings and interviews.
Follow-up activity
Create and act out another role-play about a pollution incident, choosing pollution of the land, air or water. Identify interested parties and create a script.

1 hour Pollution – a worldwide problem?

Learning objectives
● Appreciate that pollution is a problem that affects countries all over the world.
● Understand that governments set targets to try to improve environmental pollution.

What you need and preparation

Prepare and display a map of the world and make a copy of a map of the world for each small group. Make copies of photocopiable pages 138–140. You will also need a range of resources for 'Development', including maps, writing materials and recording equipment.

What to do

25 mins **Introduction**

Remind the children that pollution is a global issue. In order to see the scope of the problem they are going to look at air pollution and how it affects countries all over the world.

Hand out copies of photocopiable pages 138 and 139 and use these to introduce the topic of air pollution, explaining, with the aid of the diagram, that air pollution is a particular problem in large urban areas that have a high concentration of population and consequently large numbers of houses, traffic and factories.

Tell the children that air pollution can also be a problem in rural areas as ozone concentrations, for example, are often higher there. Ozone forms slowly as sunlight acts on oxides of nitrogen and unburnt hydrocarbons that are carried away from cities by the wind.

Use the diagram of 'Sources of acid rain: Norway' on photocopiable page 138 to discuss how pollution in one country can originate from a number of sources. Discuss some of the other statistics provided on photocopiable page 139.

Now distribute copies of photocopiable page 140 and ask the children to look at some examples of what governments across the world have done about the problem. Encourage them to try to identify some of the major causes, such as that our modern society demands and expects a high quality lifestyle and that lifestyle comes with a cost. Unfortunately the development of new and sophisticated technology has not been matched by progress in environmental protective measures.

Discuss whether governments should take even stronger measures to control industry and individuals and prevent them from harming the environment.

20 mins Development

Divide the class into small groups and give each one a blank world map. Ask them to create a world pollution map illustrating some of the places where pollution is a particular problem. They could add a sentence to each location to explain the nature of the problem and its causes.

Some groups might produce a radio broadcast from one of these locations with an interviewer describing the problem in outline and then interviewing some members of the public and business people to ask how it affects their lives.

Bring the class together to discuss their responses to the issues, and ask for reports from the radio correspondents.

15 mins Plenary

Discuss with the children whether they think this information concerns them. *How do you feel about the fact that there seem to be large parts of these environmental problems that remain unsolved? What kinds of measures would you think of taking if you had the power and authority to do something about these problems?*

Differentiation

The less able children will need help with the map exercise, locating some of the places and representing the pollution problem.

The more able could research other areas where pollution occurs, using the library or the Internet to investigate places such as Australia or India.

Assessing learning outcomes

Are the children able to appreciate how one country's individual and domestic activities can affect another? Do the children feel that the problems of pollution are sufficiently serious to warrant greater government action?

Lesson organisation
Introductory teacher-led discussion; small-group activity; whole-class discussion; plenary.

Vocabulary
quality
emissions
ozone

ICT opportunities
Produce the 'pollution' map on the computer.

Follow-up activities
● Compose letters to children in other countries asking them whether they are affected directly by the pollution in their country. Alternatively, write letters in response to someone enquiring about aspects of pollution in Great Britain.
● Carry out research to find out about other government policies on pollution and add them to the information supplied on photocopiable page 140.

CHAPTER 4

Building healthy communities

This chapter is intended to encourage the children to apply the idea of 'being healthy' to aspects of their own community, in much the same way as they might use the term to describe a person. The children will have encountered, through the media, incidents and forms of behaviour to which the terms 'healthy' or 'unhealthy' might be applied. Often, when some atrocity against a child or adult is perpetrated, our society will be described as 'sick'. However, it is equally important that children are encouraged to celebrate the 'healthy' aspects of our society's behaviour when some particularly meritorious act of kindness or goodwill is reported.

The chapter applies the term 'health' to various contexts, including places, people and organisations but, at the heart of the issue, is the fact that it is people who contribute to the healthy (or unhealthy) state of our community.

The concept of 'caring' for the health of the community is developed by exploring instances that deal with people, places, property, the past and, finally, the politics or governing of our community. The chapter develops the idea that individuals within a community share a responsibility for 'taking care' of it and, in so doing, protect the 'health' of the community. Conversely, it is also demonstrated that when people don't take any responsibility and adopt a 'couldn't-care-less' attitude, that the overall health of their society will suffer.

The chapter then links taking responsibility and caring to the process of taking decisions and making choices – about health, education, leisure, work and laws. It is through an understanding of the decisions that have to be taken that the health of our community is also protected and enhanced.

These and other concepts lie at the heart of citizenship. They incorporate an understanding of how our society works, the skills that must be applied to the process of managing our society, and the attitudes and values that help form and shape our behaviour.

Children of this age need opportunities to examine and discuss such vital issues that affect their present and future lives.

Who cares for...?

This unit explores the extent to which a community is a collection of caring people. It does this by identifying five areas to which the term 'care' can be applied – people, places, property, past (achievements) and politics.

Children of this age are likely to have begun to sense the idea of the community, either from a school, church or club perspective. They may even be aware of how other people respond to the issue of a 'caring community' – parents, friends and relatives may be active in these areas, and the children themselves may play a part.

The activities demonstrate the various ways in which the term 'care' can be defined. The first activity examines the issue of how people's lives can be affected by economic or political decisions and explores how 'interest groups' within a community represent a powerful voice in determining change.

The second activity deals with the subject of scarce resources linked to 'community' development. It challenges the children to think about priorities for action in the community and how responses to these have to be managed carefully.

The next activity looks at the whole issue of people's attitudes towards the property and possessions of others. It examines why theft, burglary and damage are such prevalent features of modern society. It introduces the idea that respect and responsibility for property are the essential ingredients: respect for others' belongings and responsibility for one's own.

This is followed by an activity that makes an attempt to look at how communities celebrate success and achievement and how this helps to build community spirit and a sense of belonging.

The final activity explores children's attitudes towards government and politics and attempts to demonstrate that everyone's life is affected by political decisions, even though they may choose to distance themselves from the system and processes.

Many of the activities involve role-play, simulation and research. Consequently the teacher's role in most of the tasks is one of co-ordination, supporting the children in the development of their personal responses to these important issues.

UNIT: Who cares for...?

Enquiry questions	Learning objectives	Teaching activities	Further teaching activities	Learning outcomes	Cross-curricular links
Who cares for... people? Do people care about the quality of other people's lives as well as their own? Are people prepared to act in the interests of other people?	● Learn that a 'healthy' community is one in which the interests of individuals and groups are respected. ● Understand that having respect for other people and their views is very important.	Talk about inconsiderate and selfish behaviour. Role-play the arguments of different groups in a community with regard to the closure of the village school.	● Look for articles in local and national newspapers that highlight behaviour that illustrates caring or non-caring behaviour by individuals or groups in a community. ● Write sample letters to a newspaper from the point of view of someone who has suffered from 'thoughtless' behaviour by another group.	*Children:* ● appreciate and value the opinions and beliefs of others from the experience of doing the role-play ● show consideration and respect for differing points of view ● translate the learning from the role-play to a real-life issue within their own community	History: preserving our heritage. Drama: role-playing.
Who cares for... places? How can a community improve the quality of its facilities for the people who live there?	● Understand that setting priorities is difficult when there is a shortage of resources. ● Recognise that decisions that conflict with one's personal views sometimes have to be accepted.	Discuss funding for local amenities and the need to prioritise. Choose projects and produce proposals for improvements.	● Produce a development plan for the area with improvement targets for the next five years. ● Prepare a newspaper article outlining the new development for the teachers.	● explain why they chose a particular proposal ● put together a convincing case for their improvement ● cope with the points of view of the committee and with rejection	English: speaking and listening – oral presentation of proposals.
Who cares for... property? How can people be encouraged to respect other people's property? How can people take more responsibility for looking after their property?	● Understand that respect for property and possessions is the sign of a healthy community. ● Appreciate that everyone has a responsibility to show respect for property.	Create and present a storyboard about a crime and its consequences. Discuss ways of dissuading criminals.	● Develop a poster and leaflet campaign to encourage children to take care of their belongings and warn them of the consequences of being careless. ● Write and produce a short play about the consequences of someone not showing respect for others' property.	● identify with the characters in the storyboard ● appreciate the various ways in which people can be influenced to change their behaviour ● handle appropriately concepts such as consequences, retribution, justice and ownership	English: writing scripts. Art and Design: creating a storyboard.
Who cares for... the past? How does success or tragedy help to create a community spirit?	● Understand that communities need to respect and learn from the past. ● Appreciate that people's present lives are affected by their past.	Research the history of the children's community to discover local achievements. Create a scrapbook of community achievements.	● Run a competition to nominate someone from the community for a special achievement. ● Organise a class or school vote. Design an award to be presented to the winner.	● readily identify topics for their scrapbook ● assess the significance of events or places ● express their personal feelings about the different topics	History: historical achievements from the past, or a local history topic.
Who cares for ... politics? How does the politics of national or local government directly affect our lives?	● Understand that politics affects people's lives whether they realise it or not. ● Appreciate that they have to decide on their own attitudes towards politics.	Hold a quiz on politics. Discuss the effects of various government policies. Role-play a debate on a particular policy.	● Carry out various political activities on behalf of the children's party such as: arrange a Party Political Broadcast; hold an election for suitable candidates for the party; produce a manifesto and other political literature.	● identify a range of consequences for the policies ● assess what parents and friends think of politics and government by what they have seen and heard ● accept the idea that their lives are affected by politics and government.	English: speaking and listening – debating a real or imaginary government policy.

Who cares for… people?

What you need and preparation

Make role cards from photocopiable page 141; you will need one card for each group. You will also need to prepare large cards for each of these groups: Parents; Teachers; Governors; Local councillors; Local shopkeepers; Local property developers; Children and Education Authority representatives. These will be used as group identification labels in the role-play.

What to do

15 mins Introduction

Introduce the focus of the lesson by asking a number of questions:
● How much do people care about the interests and well-being of particular groups within our society?
● Are people sometimes too busy with their own lives to care about what happens to others?
● Do people only begin to care and do something about a particular situation when it starts to affect them?
● Do we live in a very selfish society?

Ask the children if they have ever felt that no one was interested in what they had to say or that they couldn't get anyone to take an interest in something that concerned them.

Talk about a few examples, such as vandalism to people's property, closure of a community facility for the elderly or disabled, a threat to someone's property from road or building development or particular groups of people being attacked or threatened. Tell the children that it is often difficult to gain public support to do something about these problems. In many such cases only those who are directly affected by the problem will be prepared to act.

Ask the children to think of examples of this type of inconsiderate and selfish behaviour. There may be local instances that they could discuss.

35 mins Development

Divide the class into the same number of groups, as you have group role-play cards. Distribute the cards made from photocopiable page 141 and explain to the children that they represent groups of people living in a small village. Tell them that the local education authority has announced a plan to close the village primary school and take the children by bus to a new school in the nearest big town.

Tell the children that the cards contain some information on the particular interests, opinions and attitudes of these groups towards the closure. They should read these and think about how they would actually express them. Suggest that they also expand on the information provided with their own ideas.

Point out that each group will have its own interests and views. Some will support, others will be against, the plan. It is also possible, in some cases, that the group may be split over the issue. Ask the groups to write down their own opinions and attitudes and give them time to prepare a statement.

Explain that later, if time permits (you will probably need to allocate an extra session for this), they will be attending a 'hearing' where all the groups will express their opinions and listen to those of others. Suggest that they should try to work out what other groups might say about their opinions and prepare responses.

Explain that this type of situation often requires some form of compromise and encourage them to consider how much they would be prepared to compromise on their approach to the 'situation'.

ICT opportunities
Prepare a newspaper report on the computer of the hearing that presents the conflicting views of the various groups.

Follow-up activity
Check through local or national newspapers for other similar situations and challenge the children to devise their own role-play on the basis of what was reported.

10 mins **Plenary**
Once the individual groups have discussed, and decided on, their own 'position', hold a class discussion on how each group set about constructing its case. How were the ideas, suggestions and opinions presented and received, and how were decisions reached? Did they spend time thinking about how the 'situation' would be presented by other groups?

Ask them how they dealt with individual differences of opinion within the group. They may have disagreed about how the group should present its views, and how strongly they should represent them.

Differentiation
Less able children will need more detailed help with the role cards – provide more information and more opinions to give them a basis on which to develop further ideas. They may also need specific examples of the way in which the closure would affect each group.

The more able children might be encouraged to think of another interest group to join the role-play or consider issues on which the existing group might be divided.

Assessing learning outcomes
Are the children able to appreciate and value the opinions and beliefs of others from the experience of doing the role-play? Do they show respect and consideration for differing points of view? Can the children translate the learning from this role-play to a real-life issue within their own community?

1 hour Who cares for... places?

What you need and preparation
Prepare a map of your local village or town and the surrounding area and enlarge it to A3 size. Display this in a prominent place. Collect a few pictures of buildings or features in the town or village to act as a visual stimulus. Use photocopiable page 142 to make cards with possible improvement schemes and their costs.

What to do

15 mins **Introduction**
Introduce the idea that communities have to consider ways in which they can improve local facilities or amenities and that they have to find ways to obtain money to make these improvements. Tell the children that it is sometimes possible to obtain Lottery funding or money from other charities.

Explain that committees who have responsibility for allocating money to groups who represent worthwhile causes are often faced with very difficult choices – whether to give money, and, if so, how much, to a particular group. Tell the children that there are never sufficient funds available to meet everyone's requests and no one ever gets exactly what they ask for. Discuss the problems that this might present. The children may have some firsthand experience of these issues or be aware of them through their parents or school.

Learning objectives
● Understand that setting priorities is difficult when there is a shortage of resources.
● Recognise that decisions that conflict with one's personal views sometimes have to be accepted.

Lesson organisation
Initial teacher introduction and stimulus activity; group discussion and reporting of outcomes; whole-class discussion; plenary.

Vocabulary
priorities
opportunities
resources
scarcity
allocation
conflict

35 mins Development

Divide the class into four groups. Spread out the resources and explain that, with the aid of the map, the pictures from their community, the ideas suggested on the cards and other ideas of their own, they are going to produce three proposals to improve their local area.

Select one group to be the committee to whom the groups must present their proposals. Tell them that their task in this session is to decide on the criteria on which they will judge the bids. They must impose restraints, such as: *We only have a budget of... and we can only accept... projects.*

Tell the other groups that they must decide, by discussion, which improvement they wish to propose. Remind them that the cards made from the photocopiable sheet will offer them ideas and possible costs but that they are free to choose other ideas relevant to the local area. Stress that the committee will have a set budget.

Once each group has discussed its plan, and drawn up a proposal, give it an opportunity to make its case to the committee. Remind the children that they have to put a strong case for their chosen improvement, providing a rationale, costings, designs and ideas for funding.

After all the proposals have been heard, the committee must make a decision based on the restraints that were set. Allow them flexibility – they could accept the stipulated number of projects, or agree more projects but impose financial cuts in order to stay within their budget.

15 mins Plenary

Discuss with the class some of the general issues that arose in the group discussions – how they chose their improvement, how they decided what should be done, how much money they would need, and where it would come from. Ask the children how minority viewpoints were handled within the groups.

Discuss the selection criteria separately with the committee group and talk about whether they should publish the criteria for the benefit of the groups.

Following the presentation, talk to the groups about how well they felt their ideas had been received. Discuss the issue of money and how this affected their thinking.

Differentiation

Less able children may need help to select an appropriate idea and create a proposal. They will also need help with the costing process. Provide 'cue statements' to help them prepare their presentation, such as: *The best argument for...* or *The best piece of evidence for...*

The more able children might be able to come up with further ideas for improvements. They might also be encouraged to think of ways of making more money available for the projects.

Assessing learning outcomes

Are the children able to consider the concept of priority? Can they say why they chose a particular proposal? Can they put together a convincing case for their improvement? Are they able to cope with the points of view of the committee? Do they cope well if they are rejected or have to make cuts?

1 hour Who cares for… property?

Learning objectives
● Understand that respect for property and possessions is the sign of a healthy community.
● Appreciate that everyone has a responsibility to show respect for property.

Lesson organisation
Introductory teacher-led focus to the lesson and stimulus activity; group reporting and display of findings; whole-class discussion; plenary.

Vocabulary
possessions
property
respect
ownership
vandalism
offence
consequences
justice
retribution

What you need and preparation
Provide writing materials, including pens, pencils, highlighters, large sheets of paper for storyboards and blank A4-sized cards.

What to do

20 mins Introduction
Begin by asking the children if they have any experience of having their property or possessions stolen or damaged. Ask them about how it happened and how they felt about it: *How was it resolved?* Encourage them to explain what they did to sort out the problem: *Did you ask anyone for help?*

Talk about why some people damage or steal other people's property and what might motivate them to do these things: jealousy, anger, frustration, a sense of enjoyment at seeing others suffer, greed, or possibly need and poverty.

Ask the children whether there is anything about the way we live, the way our communities are structured, that makes vandalism and theft easier to get away with. Suggest that people don't 'look out' for each other as much as they used to and may be scared to get involved if they see criminal activity taking place.

25 mins Development
Split the class into three main groups and then smaller sub-groups to undertake the separate tasks. Before the groups begin working separately, decide together on the type of 'crime' that they will highlight in their storyboards. Encourage them to choose issues that affect them within school, such as taking or damaging other people's property. Then set the tasks for each group.

Group 1: Produce a storyboard, with text and drawings, of how a person became involved in that 'crime'. They must imagine that this is going to be the first part of a short video about how a particular person becomes involved in doing something that is wrong. Ask the group to start by 'brainstorming' all the possible reasons why this person might have become involved in this activity. Some of these ideas can then be built into the storyboard. They must try, in their drawings, to show why this person was led to perform this act.

Group 2: Produce a storyboard depicting the consequences of this person's act, imagining that it is the second part of the short video. They should show the impact of his/her behaviour on any victims.

Group 3: Produce a storyboard for the final part of the video depicting ways in which the offender could be dissuaded from continuing with this type of activity – could the children take action themselves or enlist the help of teachers? The purpose of this part of the storyboard would be to present these as strategies to prevent the person doing this again.

Allow about ten minutes at the end for the groups to present their storyboards and see how the combination would work.

15 mins Plenary
Ask the children to think about what they were trying to achieve in each of their storyboards. Talk about the techniques they have used in the storyboards to get their message across. Discuss their ideas and whether someone involved in wrongdoing would be influenced by their work. Ask the children the extent to which they think things such as videos, advertisements and poster campaigns can actually change people's behaviour.

Differentiation

Less able children will need help with the storyboards. Consider giving them the initial story and frames and asking them to complete the storyboard. Talk the ideas through with the group first, note the main points of the discussion and suggest that they use these as a guide for what they have to do.

The more able children should be able to add a commentary or character voice-overs to the storyboard as well as a 'shooting script' of locations and settings.

Assessing learning outcomes

Are the children able to identify with the offender, the victim and the person responsible for dealing with the situation? Do they appreciate the various ways in which people can be influenced to change their behaviour? How well do the children handle concepts such as consequences, justice, retribution and ownership?

> **Follow-up activity**
> Provide an opportunity for the children to act out one or more of the stories with a prepared script. If possible, film the scenes on a video camera.

Who cares for... the past?

What you need and preparation

Gather up some maps or photographs of your town or village, preferably with buildings and facilities marked. Make a collection of local newspaper articles covering a period in time that shows significant changes, perhaps 50 years. These materials should illustrate topics such as housing, transport, shopping and work. This lesson could easily be linked to work on a local history topic.

What to do

15 mins Introduction

Suggest to the class that, just like the members of a football, hockey or cricket team, a community benefits from the success its members achieve. Point out that success produces all kinds of positive feelings such as: pride, a sense of belonging, achievement, desire to be part of the success, or ambition to achieve something oneself.

Remind the children, if necessary, of how a community sometimes turns out to welcome a returning successful individual or team, such as Olympic medal winners, a triumphant football team, or even, in certain communities, successful racehorses. Ask the children: *Why do you think people do this? Why do they care?* Some of the children may have participated in a welcome like this themselves and can give their own reasons.

Point out to the children that communities also come together when unpleasant things happen. In the past mining disasters or shipwrecks brought people together but, more recently, closures of factories or the tragic death of a child have united communities. The children may be able to give examples of local incidents, or stories that reached the national headlines, and how these created a community 'spirit'. Ask the children: *What feelings would this type of incident create in people?*

35 mins Development

Divide the class into groups and outline the tasks to them. Explain that the aim is to produce a 'community scrapbook' that focuses on 'Achievements – past and present'. Tell them that the idea is to carry out research on the history of their community to find events, people, places or objects that reflect the community's achievements, things of which people can be justly proud.

They should start by using the maps and pictures to identify places. Explain that, if they

> **Learning objectives**
> ● Understand that communities need to respect and learn from the past.
> ● Appreciate that people's present lives are affected by the past.
>
> **Lesson organisation**
> Initial teacher introduction and stimulus activity; group activity, then reporting and publishing of outcomes; whole-class discussion; plenary.
>
> **Vocabulary**
> achievement
> heritage
> memory
> pride
> success
> recognition
> reward

wish, each group can take responsibility for a particular time period or a particular topic, so one could concentrate on events (past and present), one could research people (individuals, teams or local organisations), another might research places, and so on.

Tell the groups that they will need to find out information any way they can – from family, school, relatives, friends, the library, newspapers or the Internet. They should also try to get hold of pictures to illustrate their topic or, if this is not possible, draw or paint the place or event. They may even be able to interview key people involved in the events or well-known people who made the headlines. They may also be able to photograph tangible 'evidence' of these achievements if any exist in the community. If there are cases where the event or person made the national headlines it may be possible to traces these records too.

Encourage the children to develop a plan of how to do the task and the time it will take. The plan could probably be prepared in one session but carrying it out will depend on time availability.

🕙 Plenary
10 mins

The discussion should revolve around what each group has achieved so far. They should report what they have done and what they are going to do next. Encourage the children to talk about any problems they have encountered when researching the past.

Ask them to report any interesting, surprising, or puzzling pieces of information, any unusual facts and good or bad news. They should also express their feelings towards what they found out. *Did you feel a sense of pride, respect or surprise?* Ask the children to talk about any responses they have had from people they talked to: *What were their reactions to the achievements?*

Differentiation

Less able children will need help to select a topic and with the research. You may need to adjust the scale of the activity accordingly. You may also need to suggest headings to help them present it.

More able children could perhaps take two examples from different times and compare the achievements.

Assessing learning outcomes

Are the children able to readily identify topics for their scrapbook? Can they assess the significance of these events or places? Can they express their personal feelings about the different topics?

Follow-up activity
It may be possible to have the children's work displayed in some public place, such as the local library, church, secondary school, community hall or in the window of a local store. The local newspaper might also be interested. Alternatively, prepare a display for the next Parents' Evening or Governors' meeting at the school.

① Who cares for... politics?
hour

Learning objectives
● Understand that politics affects people's lives whether they realise it or not.
● Appreciate that they have to decide on their own attitude towards politics.

Lesson organisation
Initial teacher-led introduction and stimulus activity; group role-plays; whole-class discussion; plenary.

What you need and preparation

Prepare 12 questions about the current Government and Opposition to give to the children as a quiz. It should not be just a 'names and places' test, but also check what each party represents in their minds. It might start by asking for the name of the prime minister and the name of the opposition leader, but go on to ask about particular policies, perhaps on current topics such as Europe, or education and schools. The purpose of this is to test how much the children know about people in politics. Prepare cards with examples of current government policies or other fictitious issues that will be of interest to the children, such as extending the school day until 5pm.

What to do

Introduction

(15 mins) Introduce the lesson by asking the children how important they think politics and the work of the Government is to their lives. You will probably find that they think that politics is something for adults to worry about! National politics is likely to be more familiar to them than local politics because of media coverage, unless there is a big local issue currently under debate.

The children may have experience of hearing adults talk about their views on politics and politicians. They may have formed opinions through listening to politicians speak on television, watching programmes about the work of the Government, even taking part locally in politics.

Ask them first if they feel that the Government and politics has anything to do with them. Then ask: *Can you think of anything the Government does that directly affects you?* You may need to put some word clues on the board – good ones to start with would be school, health or leisure. Other words (such as work or transport) might encourage them to think a little harder!

Try the prepared quiz on the whole class to test their knowledge of the present system and the party and individuals currently in power.

Development

(35 mins) Divide the class into pairs or threes and explain that they are going to play a game of 'consequences'. Explain that you will give each group a card with a government policy, perhaps that all cyclists should take a test before they are allowed to ride on the road or that smoking will be banned in all public places. Tell them that when they receive the policy they have four minutes in which to write down the 'consequences' of that policy for themselves.

When this has been done combine two groups and explain that they will now be doing a role-play exercise. One half of the group will play the role of the people who would be affected by the policy, while the other half play the role of the Government and defend the policy. They should take turns to be on both sides and deal with both policies.

Following the role-play discussion, the Government part of the group should consider making amendments to the policy in the light of the comments of the lobbying group.

Plenary

(10 mins) Ask one group to present the consequences they have identified for one particular policy. Encourage them to explain their reasoning.

Talk about policies for which it was particularly difficult to identify consequences for themselves: *Why was this the case?* (This may apply to policies on road transport or labelling and packaging food.) Try to push the consequences of one of these as far as possible in the plenary session.

Differentiation

The less able children may need a quiz that is adapted from the main one. They will also need help with the consequences game and could be given one or two picture cards as clues to get them started. Alternatively, restrict the type and range of policies they have to consider.

More able children could take an example of how a policy in one area, such as education or health, affects other areas of life.

Assessing learning outcomes

Can the children identify a range of consequences for the policies? Are they able to assess what parents and friends think of politics and government from what they have seen and heard? Are they able to accept the idea that politics and government affect their lives? Do they make valid personal responses to the importance of government?

Vocabulary
government
council
parliament
election
representative
opposition
politics

Follow-up activity
Choose one of the policies to debate in class with the children in role as the Government and the Opposition.

BUILDING HEALTHY COMMUNITIES

Who decides about...?

This unit is intended to help the children understand how decisions are taken about particular aspects of their own lives, and of the lives of others who are close to them. Children are often unsure of who makes some of the decisions that affect their lives and the processes involved. This applies to quite familiar contexts such as school, and routine decisions such as who decides they should attend, who decides how much money is spent and who chooses the teachers?

In this unit the subjects of health, education, work, leisure and laws are taken as the contexts in which the children can explore the key questions of: Who decides? How do they decide? What decisions do they take? In what way, if any, can people affect those decisions?

Involvement in decision-making is often made an important part of the school community, through pupil councils and other forms of democratic process. These processes not only help the children to understand the reasoning and rationale behind making good decisions, but they also help them to form positive attitudes towards democratic decision-making.

This area of the curriculum is the arena in which children can exercise their knowledge and skills, and also begin to shape attitudes of duty, responsibility, and an obligation to contribute to their own community. Indifference is shown to be one of the main reasons why our society often displays apathy towards politics and government.

The message that lies at the heart of these themes and activities is the importance of involvement. If such ideas are offered to young children, and fostered and nurtured through the school, they will carry them forward as the next generation of community decision-makers.

UNIT: Who decides about...?

Enquiry questions	Learning objectives	Teaching activities	Further teaching activities	Learning outcomes	Cross-curricular links
Who decides about... our health Who makes decisions about health provision in our society? How can decisions about health be changed or influenced by those who are directly affected by them?	● Understand that decisions about our health are made at many different levels of national and local government. ● Appreciate that decisions can be influenced and changed at each of those levels.	Discuss the health service and its funding. Consider different health-related decisions and the difficulty of prioritising.	● Create a news report for radio or television about a 'local' health issue that is of interest to listeners. ● Set up a simulated radio phone-in with someone representing the health authority and allow the rest of the class to ask questions and present their point of view on the issue as 'interested' parties.	*Children:* ● appreciate the levels of decision-making, relating to health provision, from government onwards ● relate this to their own experiences of the health service at any level ● appreciate the difficulties associated with making good decisions in a health service where resources are limited	Health education: people who take care of our health.
Who decides about... our education? What are the different levels of government at which decisions about education are taken? How do the decisions taken about education affect people's lives?	● Understand that decisions about our education are made at many different levels, and by many different individuals. ● Appreciate that it may be possible to influence and change these decisions.	Talk about the people who make decisions on education. Role-play a debate on an educational decision.	● Design a curriculum for a day or week. What would you include? ● Design a curriculum for parents. What would you put in it?	● appreciate how many different groups are involved in decision-making for education ● understand the problems associated with making good educational decisions with limited resources	English: speaking and listening – debating educational issues.
Who decides about... our work? How can the concept of 'work' be defined? How easy is it to match the right person to the right job?	● Understand that decisions about work opportunities are made at many different levels. ● Appreciate that these decisions can often be very difficult to assess.	Write job applications and carry out interviews. Discuss the problems involved in making and accepting difficult decisions.	● Write out a description of an 'ideal' job for the future - what would it entail, where would it be, would you work on your own? ● Write an advertisement to persuade someone else why this job is ideal.	● appreciate the different processes involved in decision-making when it is done by a group rather than just one person ● express feelings about success and failure ● appreciate the difficulties associated with making good decisions when not all the information is available	English: writing job applications.
Who decides about... our leisure? What forms of leisure facilities are appropriate for a community? How are priority decisions taken when resources are scarce?	● Understand that resources and funding for leisure facilities come from many different sources. ● Appreciate that the needs and interests of the whole community must be taken into account when decisions are made.	Discuss funding for leisure facilities. Produce and present a proposal for a new local leisure facility.	● Design a poster to promote a local leisure facility for a particular age group. ● Design a questionnaire to gather information about local people's opinions on the level and quality of leisure facilities.	● appreciate how decisions related to sports and leisure activities are made ● appreciate that resources for leisure facilities may be scarce and that makes the decision-making process more complex	English: oral presentation of proposals.
Who decides about... our laws? How is respect for the law encouraged and promoted? How do children form and uphold laws within their own groups?	● Understand that laws are necessary to help us live co-operatively. ● Appreciate that laws must be practical and benefit the whole community.	Talk about laws and law enforcement. Propose and present new or improved laws.	● Produce a small illustrated booklet for young children explaining one particular law which applies to them, using suitable text and illustrations. ● Produce a 'did you know that' guide to the law for young people.	● understand how laws are made ● understand why laws are necessary ● appreciate that a level of compromise may be required in law-making.	English: oral presentation of proposed new laws.

1 hour   Who decides about... our health?

What you need and preparation

Prepare a series of decision/suggestion cards for group work containing a list of health-related decisions, such as: *The local council has decided to close down a day centre for disabled people*; *The Government has decided to increase the amount people have to pay for their prescriptions*; *A local doctor has suggested that, in his opinion, people who smoke should be charged more for medical help.*

You will also need card, paper and pens for recording the group work and access to a board or flipchart.

What to do

20 mins Introduction

Introduce the topic of healthcare to the children by asking about the various forms of care they have experienced. Ask if they know who makes the decisions and provides the funding for these services. Explain the process, starting with decisions made at government level, then by local authorities, and then by professionals at clinics and hospitals. Work through to the individual who, in the last resort, can decide to act or not on what is offered.

Explain that funding comes from the government through the taxes people pay and that the money is then allocated to councils to spend on health care. Tell the children that there are two systems – a public (national) health service and also a private health service. Explain the differences.

Ask the children to talk in greater detail about any parts of the health system they have had experience of. Some may mention hospitals, specialists, or visiting a doctor, dentist or nurse at a surgery. Try to find as many examples as possible from the children's experiences. Some children may be able to talk about how quickly (or not) they received treatment and how well (or not) they were looked after.

Suggest that, at the end of the chain of decision-making on their health, they may have had to make decisions themselves – Did they take the medicine? Do they do any exercise? Do they clean their teeth? and so on. *On what did you base these decisions?*

Conclude by raising the issue of resources and how a shortage of these creates problems for the people who look after the health of the nation. A lack of money, people, space, time and equipment makes it difficult to provide an efficient health service. Explain about having to work to a limited budget – there are things you can do and things you can't. In this situation the difficulty is that it can be a matter of life and death.

(25 mins) Development

Divide the class into groups and give each group one decision/suggestion card. Explain that their task is to find three reasons why they think that decision or suggestion was made (the benefits) and three reasons why they think the decision or suggestion is not a good one (the costs and disadvantages). They should also try to come up with three alternative suggestions, that offer a compromise and one person, or group from whom they would try to get support for this compromise.

Tell them that each group should record their decisions and, at the end of the decision-making discussion, all the groups will come together and briefly present their findings. Give the children time to respond to what the other groups have said. Then, as a whole class, take one group's findings and discuss the issues and suggestions. *Do the benefits outweigh the disadvantages? How workable are the compromises? Would you get the support you need?*

Depending on the time available, swap decision cards and repeat the process.

(15 mins) Plenary

Talk about the problems involved in making difficult decisions such as enforcing them once they have been made and explaining them to people who find them hard to accept. Introduce issues such as taking people off life-support systems or withholding medication, and the difficult decisions doctors have to make about keeping people alive or donating the organs of people who have died.

Ask the children if they have ever had to accept a decision that they thought was wrong. *How was it explained to them? What did you think of the explanation? How did you feel about having to accept it?* How do they feel, for instance, about people who do not allow their children to have surgery because it conflicts with their religious beliefs?

Discuss how they would vote if the government wanted to give hospitals the authority to use the organs from people who have died to save other people.

Differentiation

Less able children will need some simpler decisions and may require one or two clues to help them get started with their response. Illustrations and drawings will help to get some of the more difficult ideas across.

More able children could discuss or write their viewpoint on euthanasia.

Assessing learning outcomes

Are the children able to appreciate the levels of decision-making relating to health provision from the government onwards? Can they relate it to their own experiences of the health service at any level? Can they appreciate the difficulties associated with making good decisions in a health service where resources such as money and people are limited?

Follow-up activity
Carry out a survey in school, at home or with other friends, on one or more of the issues discussed, such as euthanasia, organ donation or personal beliefs and values determining the outcome of someone else's life.

Who decides
about...?

1 hour Who decides about... our education?

Learning objectives
● Understand that decisions about our education are made at many different levels and by many different individuals.
● Appreciate it may be possible to influence and change these decisions.

Lesson organisation
Initial teacher introduction and stimulus activity; group role-plays and presentations of outcomes; whole-class discussion; plenary.

What you need and preparation
Prepare cards labelled with the various working groups which are active within an educational setting – headteacher, governors, parents, local business people, education advisors, teachers. You will also need a series of cards with suggestions or decisions relating to a school situation. Some suggestions are provided on photocopiable page 143 but you may wish to provide others.

Paper and writing materials will be required for reporting the group decisions.

What to do

20 mins Introduction
Talk to the children about the decision-making process related to education. In your explanation, discuss the roles of the headteacher, governors, parents, local business people, education advisors and teachers. Point out that many decisions are first made by the Government but then move through the process down to the individual who is affected by them. Explain that people are then free to accept or reject the education that is offered to them, but point out that few people choose to educate their own children outside the school system.

Ask the children if they can think of education decisions that have affected them – not just those taken by their school, but others made by the government, such as the Literacy Hour, or by the local authority, such as those related to transport or meals. Choose one example and ask the children how they felt about the decision.

Point out that they may be able to affect the decision in some way – by accepting it, by accepting part of it, even rejecting it. Try to help them think of examples. Talk about the shortage

Vocabulary
representation
debate
consultation
dialogue
negotiation
management

of resources (money, staff, space, time, equipment and so on) that creates a problem for the people who are responsible for the education of the nation. Discuss the difficulties and frustrations of having to work to a limited budget.

30 mins Development

Divide the class into enough groups for there to be one representing each group of people on the cards and assign them their roles. Select one of the decision or suggestion cards. Tell the 'headteacher' group that they are in favour of this idea and that they should choose one member to act as spokesperson.

Advise the other groups that they should choose whether they support the idea or reject it. Tell them that complete groups do not have to agree unanimously – parents, for example, may be divided in their opinions.

Allow them a little time to discuss their views, then invite the headteacher spokesperson to introduce the decision or suggestion, supported, if necessary, by the group. Give each of the other groups a chance to state their points of view, either as a group or as individuals.

After each group has stated their point of view on the suggested idea, there should be an opportunity for the headteacher, and possibly other staff, to respond, and for the particular group to come back with additional comments.

10 mins Plenary

Talk about making and justifying difficult decisions. In a school context this could relate to not selecting someone to take part in a play or a team, or not allowing children to do certain activities at break or lunchtime.

Ask the children to talk about their own experiences of having to accept decisions that affected them but which they were not allowed to influence. Did they think this was unfair? Talk about compromise – that people often have to give something up in order to get something else. *Has this ever happened to you?*

If you do not already have one, ask the children how useful they think it would be to have a pupil committee to represent their views to the teachers, the head and the governors. If you do have an existing system talk about how effectively it operates.

Differentiation

Less able children will need simpler decisions or suggestions and may benefit from one or two clues to get them started on their response. Illustrations and drawings will help get some of the more difficult ideas across.

More able children might be challenged to construct a 'Pupils' Charter' for consideration by the staff and headteacher.

Assessing learning outcomes

Do the children appreciate how many different groups are involved in decision-making for education? Do they understand the problems associated with making good educational decisions with limited resources?

Follow-up activity
Interview representatives of the groups, in role, about their views on changes to the school curriculum or the structure of schools. Try to identify how the decision would affect that individual and whether he or she would feel able to accept it.

①hour Who decides about... our work?

Learning objectives
● Understand that decisions about work opportunities are made at many different levels.
● Appreciate that these decisions can often be very difficult to assess.

Lesson organisation
Initial teacher introduction and stimulus activity; group role-plays; whole-class discussion; plenary.

What you need and preparation
Make a copy of photocopiable page 144 for each group. Alternatively, prepare a number of similar partly-completed job advertisements. The children will also need writing materials.

What to do

⑮mins Introduction
Talk about work and job creation to the children and discuss the decisions that have to be made by the Government regarding support and resources. Explain the process, starting with government policy about employment, discussing various businesses and employers and finishing with the individual who has to decide whether or not to accept a job.

Ask the children about their understanding of the different uses of the word 'work', such as: paid employment, voluntary work, a 'job', a 'vocation' or a 'career'. Discuss the different emphases and encourage the children to relate these to any experiences of their own – they may have friends or family members who choose to work for different reasons..

Conclude by talking about the difficulties facing people who are looking for work – lack of job opportunities, problems with travelling to new work opportunities, lack of qualifications or skills, and so on.

㉚mins Development
Divide the class into groups, then ask each group to divide into two sub-groups. Explain that one half is employers and the other half applicants.

Give each group of employers a copy of photocopiable page 144 (or one of your own partly-finished job advertisements) and tell them that their task is to complete it. They should list all the relevant knowledge, skills and personal details they would need to know.

Meanwhile the applicants must try to work out what the employers will be asking for in the completed advertisement. They should also select one member to be interviewed for the job by the employers.

Vocabulary
work
vocation
job
career
satisfaction
money
prospects
promotion

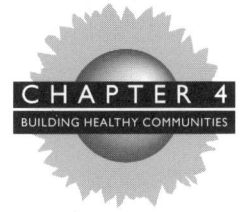
Give the employers about ten minutes to interview the candidate, then ask them to decide whether they would give the job to that person. If not, they should indicate why they have made that decision.

⏱ **15 mins** Plenary

Review discussions from other lessons about making difficult decisions, accepting them once they have been made and explaining them to other people, who may find them hard to accept. Indicate how this applies to choosing applicants or interviewing for a job. Ask the children: *How easy was it for the 'applicant' group to select a candidate? How easy was it for the 'employer' group to select a candidate? How did the unsuccessful candidates feel?*

Talk about accepting unpleasant decisions. How did the unsuccessful candidates feel about the employers' explanation for them not being appointed?

Differentiation
Less able children may need some clues in the form of words or phrases, such as: *a good speaking voice*, or, *must enjoy working with children*, to help them complete the photocopiable sheet.

More able children could add other criteria to those listed on the photocopiable sheet.

Assessing learning outcomes
Do the children appreciate the different processes involved in decision-making when it is done by a group rather than just one person? Can they express feelings about success and failure? Do they appreciate the difficulties associated with making good decisions when not all the information is available?

⏱ **1 hour** Who decides about... our leisure?

What you need and preparation
Make copies of photocopiable pages 145 and 146 for each group. You will also need to provide writing materials for group work.

What to do

⏱ **20 mins** Introduction
Introduce the topic of leisure and recreation to the children, explaining how national and local government policy can affect the individual's leisure activities, through the availability of money, staff and premises. The discussion could also cover sponsorship and finance of sport by industry, or Lottery funding. Ask the children if they know of any specific examples of businesses sponsoring sport. They are likely to mention motor racing, football, snooker or cricket, and the issue of tobacco sponsorship will probably arise. Distribute photocopiable page 145 and use this to promote the discussion.

Talk to the children about the level and type of leisure and recreational facilities in their area and ask if they know of any examples of different types of funding of the local sports and

Who decides about...?

Vocabulary
leisure
recreation
facilities
resources
space
finance
sport
relaxation

leisure facilities. This may be an opportunity to talk about the provision of other leisure facilities, such as libraries, theatre, cinema and parks. *Do you think that the facilities are the right ones? Are there enough? Do you use them?*

Discuss the difficulty of prioritising time and resources for sport and other leisure activities. Invite the headteacher to join the session so that the children can ask about the PE and Games included in school time and about some of the difficult choices that have to be made. These will include asking parents or parent-teacher associations to provide their time and money to help with sport (and other extra-curricular activities).

(25 mins) Development

Divide the class into groups and explain that each group is to produce a proposal for a new leisure facility in their area. This could be a sports centre, or a leisure facility such as an arts and craft gallery where everyone from the community could display their work. Give each group a copy of photocopiable page 146 and read through the headings under which they should write their proposal. Explain that they need to get across their basic idea, justify the need for it and who would use it, why it would benefit the community as a whole and where it might be located.

After their discussion each group should produce a five-minute oral presentation of their proposal to present to an impartial assessor. Encourage the children to use drawings to support their proposal and show evidence that they have researched their idea by talking to classmates and considering the needs and interests of parents and other adults.

(15 mins) Plenary

Talk about prioritising and making difficult decisions. Relate this to the topic of providing leisure facilities within a town and the problem of satisfying a majority of people. Ask the children to think of any groups or individuals in the community who might oppose their proposal. *What might the opponents say? How would you respond to their criticism or objections?*

Discuss whether the children have ever been denied something that they really wanted to do. They may have examples from school or youth club where they have been told that they could not use a particular facility or piece of equipment. Ask them how they felt about this.

Ask about ways of compromising in this type of situation. *Would you be prepared to give up your time and energy to help the school to get a facility, perhaps sports or drama equipment?*

ICT opportunities
Develop the proposal on the computer. Include drawings, diagrams, maps and charts related to the facility.

Follow-up activities
● Invite a local councillor to talk to the children about how decisions are taken on the provision of leisure facilities and how the needs of the community are met.
● Write to friends or pen-pals to ask them about the level of leisure facilities in their school or community.

Differentiation

Less able children will need specific help with the proposal, particularly with identifying the need for the facility.

More able children could take one of the proposals and draft an imaginary response from their local council.

Assessing learning outcomes

Are the children able to appreciate how decisions related to sports and leisure activities are made? Do they appreciate that resources for leisure facilities may be scarce and that makes the decision-making process more complex?

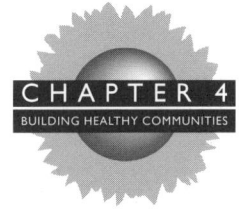
① Who decides about... our laws?
hour

What you need and preparation
Make several copies of photocopiable page 147. You will also need to provide writing materials for group work.

What to do

⓴ Introduction
mins
Talk about laws and law enforcement to the children, explaining how the law-making process works and where the balance of power lies. Use photocopiable page 147 as a stimulus for a discussion about attitudes to the law.

Encourage the children to talk about specific laws that directly affect them. They may mention going to school, the films they are allowed to see at the cinema or buying certain items, such as cigarettes or alcohol. Ask them whether they feel the laws are good and sensible. *Why do you think that law was introduced?*

㉚ Development
mins
Divide the class into groups and explain that each group has a choice. They can either take an existing law that affects them, but which they do not agree with, and suggest how it could be changed – or choose a subject about which they think a new law should be drafted.

Ask the children to provide as many reasons as possible for the proposed changes and encourage them to look for reasons that people other than themselves might offer. They should describe how they feel the new law would benefit the community as a whole, as well as considering how feasible it would be to apply it. *What might happen if people broke your law?*

After some preparation time each group should make a five-minute presentation of their proposed law. Ask the rest of the class to comment on each one and, if necessary, suggest additions or modifications. The groups could then, in the light of the comments, redraft their law.

⑩ Plenary
mins
Talk to the children about having to accept laws that are made on their behalf. Encourage them to talk about rules at home, or in school, and how they feel about them. Do they accept them as necessary and sensible?

Talk to the children about how they make rules for their own games or other activities. *How do you try to create and explain the rules? How do you deal with people who don't follow the rules?*

Introduce the topic of compromise and ask to what degree they accept that they may have to compromise in order to play co-operatively.

Differentiation
Less able children will need help to select a law. Suggest a few ideas such as changing the legal age for seeing certain films, buying cigarettes, or riding a motorcycle.

More able children could be asked to consider a law for an older age range, perhaps in connection with driving a car, or borrowing money from a bank.

Assessing learning outcomes
Do the children understand how laws are made? Do they understand why laws are necessary? Do they appreciate that a level of compromise may be required in law-making?

Learning objectives
● Understand that laws are necessary to help us live cooperatively.
● Appreciate that laws must be practical and benefit the whole community.

Lesson organisation
Initial teacher introduction and stimulus activity; group discussions and presentations of outcomes; whole-class discussion; plenary.

Vocabulary
law
legislation
courts
legal
illegal
crime
punishment
prison

ICT opportunities
Draft response letters from the public to the proposed law on the computer.

Follow-up activities
● Research laws that have affected children from Victorian times to the present day and produce a visual representation of the changes.
● Investigate how laws affect children in other countries.

CHAPTER 5

Building a healthy future

Helping children to think about aspects of the future of their society is an important dimension of the PSHE curriculum. Encouraging children to think, for instance, about how to achieve greater justice and equality for the various groups within our society is a valuable learning experience. It is important that children think of themselves as people who will not only help shape the society of the future but will also be the recipients of that fairness and justice from other sources.

Helping children to identify inequalities in the way our society treats particular groups is an important part of the citizenship agenda. This chapter looks at inequality from the perspectives of wealth, work, health and law and order. This is a particularly sensitive area since some of the children and their families will themselves be the victims of that inequality. It is vital, however, that causes and consequences of inequality are examined and discussed in an objective manner. It is also crucial that emphasis is placed on the positive steps that are being taken to rectify inequality.

Assisting children to consider some of the important, but changing, issues that will face future societies, such as technology, leisure and work, is also an important objective for PSHE. It is part of helping children to appreciate the responsibility that they will share with others for the shape and direction which their society will take. It is important that they develop a sense of responsibility for aspects of their own lives and they can begin this process by exploring how, even at this age, they can influence, at least in part, some of the ways in which their own community develops. It is vital that children do not adopt the 'couldn't-care-less' or 'it's-nothing-to-do-with-me' attitudes which bedevil attempts to engage people in shaping their own future.

The activities in this chapter are intended to help sensitise children to the important role that they will need to play in the future development of their society.

A just and fair society

This unit invites the children to consider the concepts of justice and fairness as they apply to our society and to imagine how they might be applied in the society of the future. Good citizenship is founded upon an appreciation of the need to protect the weak and disadvantaged, to ensure civil, political and social justice and to promote respect for the law. In this unit these concepts are investigated in a range of different topic areas.

The first of these topics is wealth and poverty – one of the major areas to which ideas of justice and fairness can be applied. The children are asked to consider the various ways in which wealth can be acquired and then apply the principles of fairness and justice to those methods. Although personal values and attitudes will have a bearing on their opinions of this subject it is important that the children's attitudes and values, whether positive or negative, are examined and evaluated.

Work, or the absence of it, is also an area through which the nature of fairness and justice can be explored. Many children and their families will be affected by the underlying economic trends within their community, so this subject should be handled sensitively. Nevertheless, it is important that the children are given an opportunity to discuss the role and purpose of all aspects of work.

There has been a recent move to educate and encourage people to consider their health and personal lifestyle carefully to ensure that they enjoy a long and healthy life. Children also need to be helped to form sound judgements about what is, and is not, good for them in matters of health and well-being.

The final lesson deals with equality of opportunity for men and women and questions how fairly this issue is dealt with in our society. It allows the children an opportunity to investigate their own, and others', attitudes to this important subject.

Learning is a lifelong process and is acquired in a variety of contexts. This unit demonstrates to children the importance of learning, from all the many experiences they have, in and out of school, and at home. It also shows them how, in the process, those experiences shape them as individuals and members of a community.

Unit: A just and fair society

Enquiry questions	Learning objectives	Teaching activities	Further teaching activities	Learning outcomes	Cross-curricular links
How do we define wealth and poverty? How do wealth and poverty shape people's lives?	● Understand that inequality may be characterised by extremes of wealth and poverty. ● Recognise that inequality creates division in terms of opportunity and life chances.	Discuss the concept of wealth and poverty. Produce a storyboard for a short television programme on the subject of 'wealth and poverty in our society'.	● Imagine that you won £1 million. What would you do with it? Think about doing without! ● Decide on priorities if money is short and you have to cut back on certain items. What would you find hardest to do without? ● Illustrate the concepts of wealth and poverty in a poster, adding key text if necessary.	*Children:* ● appreciate the different dimensions to the idea of wealth ● appreciate the various attitudes people have towards wealth and poverty ● discuss issues of fairness, justice and fair play in this context	Geography: poverty in developing countries. English/Art and Design: producing a storyboard.
Why do people work? What forms of work are found in our society?	● Understand that people have a variety of reasons for working and not working. ● Recognise that the presence (or absence) of work affects everyone in our society.	List people's reasons for choosing to work. Produce a leaflet or poster promoting a particular job.	● Look at job advertisements in newspapers and decide what the attractions (or otherwise) of that job would be. ● Choose a job and mime aspects of it to the group to enable them to guess what it is.	● discuss different ideas of what constitutes work ● appreciate the benefits of work to the individual and society ● express their views and opinions on the reasons why people choose to avoid regular work	Art and Design: creating a leaflet or poster.
How do we define the terms 'healthy' and 'unhealthy'? How does inequality in terms of society's resources affect people's lives?	● Understand that people's health depends on the choices they are able to make. ● Appreciate that many people live in societies where their choices are limited.	Explore health issues in developing countries. Visualise and draw a picture of some of this information.	● Debate the statement that 'Out of sight is out of mind' when it relates to the suffering of people in other parts of the world. ● Develop strategies to appeal to other people to help children in other countries who are suffering. ● Design a card which carries information and images related to the theme.	● appreciate that the world is a place of inequality ● appreciate that everyone has a responsibility to help alleviate suffering, even in a small way	Geography: health concerns in developing countries. Art and Design: creating a poster.
Why do people break the laws of our society? How does crime affect both the criminal and the victim?	● Understand that people may exhibit lawful or unlawful behaviour. ● Develop notions of justice.	Write and perform a short play on the unfairness of crime. Discuss the issues raised.	● Design a storyboard covering the theme of young children and crime. ● Design and draft rules for children in school.	● link crime or unlawful behaviour with unfairness and inequality ● identify with the issue on a personal level	English: writing a short play. Drama: performing a short play.
What is equality of opportunity? How does it apply to the topic of gender?	● Learn that equality of opportunity, in terms of gender, is a major issue within our society. ● Appreciate that attitudes towards equal opportunities can be complex.	Discuss inequality. Create illustrated literature that promotes equal opportunities.	● Show children in other classes, parents and friends photocopiable page 156 and record their 'instant' responses. ● Look for articles in the press or reports on television of issues associated with equality of opportunity. ● Look at equality of opportunity from the perspective of race.	● appreciate the different areas in which inequality often occurs ● discuss and evaluate the reasons why inequality exists ● relate aspects of this topic to their own participation in the activity.	Art and Design: creating a poster.

① How do we define wealth and poverty?

What you need and preparation

Collect some pictures or photographs of objects depicting aspects of wealth, including a large house, an expensive car or a yacht. These will be used as stimulus for a discussion about the concept of wealth. You will also need pictures or photographs depicting aspects of poverty, including poor housing and undernourished or homeless people.

Prepare copies of photocopiable pages 148 and 149, as well as recording sheets for the children's group work, entitled *What is wealth?*. You will also need writing materials and access to a board or flipchart.

What to do

⑳ Introduction

Introduce the concept of wealth by asking the children what kinds of things they associate with 'wealth'. List their responses on the board. Their suggestions will probably relate to material wealth, as represented by houses, cars, boats, land, and so on. Distribute copies of photocopiable page 148 and ask the children, in pairs, to add items to the picture which, in their opinion, would signify that the family was wealthy.

Follow up this activity by raising the question of how these people might have acquired such wealth – from work, inheritance, winnings, savings or investments. Explore the children's attitudes to extreme wealth – this may raise questions of fairness, justice and fair play. How do they feel about the fact that some people get paid huge salaries while others have to work very hard for comparatively little? Some people spend a lifetime accumulating wealth, while others inherit wealth in a family business or buy one lottery ticket and become millionaires.

Now ask the children what they associate with the word 'poverty'. Again, list their responses on the board. Ask if they know why some people find themselves living in poverty – this may be the result of the loss of a job, an inadequate education, the lack of a permanent home, no family support or they may be refugees. Hand out copies of photocopiable page 149 and discuss the statements with the children, identifying causes and consequences for the facts given.

㉕ Development

Divide the class into groups of about six children and introduce the task. Each group has to imagine that it has the opportunity to produce a short television programme on the subject of wealth and poverty in our society. They should tackle the following parts of the task in this order:

● Decide what messages about wealth and poverty they want to give. Will it be highly critical of the wealthy? What will it say about those in poverty? Will it try to create a balanced viewpoint?

● Decide what aspects of society they will show to illustrate the extremes of wealth and poverty – perhaps a family in one part of a city with a large house and car, while two miles away there lives a homeless family.

● Decide what facts they should present to illustrate their ideas of wealth and poverty.

Once they have planned these elements, the group could subdivide, take one element each, and develop their ideas on how it should be portrayed in the film. They should consider aspects such as the visuals, the script, the opinions and viewpoints. Explain the importance of the sub-groups reporting to each other on what they have done so that the whole group remains aware of the different inputs to the 'production'. Encourage the children to look at their own local environment for any illustrative material.

The group should then work together to produce a simple storyboard of their programme,

Learning objectives
● Understand that inequality may be characterised by extremes of wealth and poverty.
● Recognise that inequality creates division in terms of opportunity and life chances.

Lesson organisation
Initial teacher-led, whole-class discussion; paired and group activities; whole-class discussion; plenary.

Vocabulary
opportunity
wealth
inequality
poverty
generosity
empathy

pulling all the elements together to show the development of their ideas.

Encourage each group to think of a title for their programme that would attract viewers' attention and provide a simple outline of what the programme is trying to achieve. They should also think about who their audience might be and at what time their programme should be screened.

15 mins Plenary

Ask the children to discuss whether this activity has produced changes in their own opinions and attitudes towards justice, fair play and equality. Allow them to make their own personal responses to these ideas and be careful to act only as a chairperson, avoiding the urge to lead the discussion to a desired outcome.

Discuss other possible interpretations of wealth and poverty – especially those that are not related to material things. Talk about wealth in terms of generosity, kindness or empathy – the qualities a person possesses – and that poverty can be the absence of such qualities. This is a more difficult area but worth tackling.

Differentiation

The less able children will require some help with planning and will need sub-headings for the overall themes of wealth and poverty and some concrete examples to get them started.

The more able children could take responsibility for scripting the programme.

Assessing learning outcomes

Do the children appreciate the different dimensions to the idea of wealth? Are they able to appreciate the various attitudes people have towards wealth and poverty? Can they discuss issues of fairness, justice and fair play in this context?

Follow-up activities
● Plan a survey to put to the people who watched the programme about their personal opinions and attitudes towards wealth and poverty. Compose three questions on the subject.
● Consider the family in photocopiable page 148 and follow their imaginary fortunes over a period of ten years.

1 hour Why do people work?

What you need and preparation

Make, enlarge, and laminate the pictures from photocopiable page 150 to use as stimulus in the Introduction. You will also need a board or flipchart, writing materials, and recording sheets for group work.

What to do

20 mins Introduction

Introduce the question of why people choose to work. List all the reasons the children offer on the board. They may suggest that it is for money, for future career progress, for stimulation and companionship, or to develop skills. Use the pictures from photocopiable page 150 to prompt their thoughts.

Develop the idea that some people work for rewards other than money – and that, in fact, some work for no money at all. Discuss the reasons these people have for working and invite the children to express their opinions of such people. They may feel sympathy for some, but be very critical of others – they may even express the view that people who work for no pay are not doing a particularly worthwhile job. Values expressed outside school may influence their views.

Ask the children for their thoughts on why some people don't work – some have no choice, they may be unwell or unqualified, some can find no suitable work in their area and others may deliberately try to avoid work. Explore the reasons why some people may prefer not to work

Learning objectives
● Understand that people have a variety of reasons for working and not working.
● Recognise that the presence (or absence) of work affects everyone in our society.

Lesson organisation
Initial teacher-led, whole-class discussion; small-group activity and publishing of the learning; whole-class discussion; plenary.

with the children and invite them to offer their opinions on this.

Ask them what they think the implications might be for our society if a lot of people choose not to work. Conclude this section by discussing the issue of fairness and justice in terms of people who take more than they give. Discuss the concept of balance and fairness in people contributing as much as they are able to.

Vocabulary
work
jobs
employment
unemployment
labour
incentive
motive

(25 mins) Development

Divide the class into groups of about four and tell them that each group must choose a particular type of work, career or job – perhaps one that they know something about because of friends, parents, or other relations.

Explain that their task is to produce a leaflet or poster that describes the type of work involved, giving examples of some of the different tasks required and the challenges and experiences the person will meet. They should then go on to list the knowledge, skills and qualities needed to do that job and explain the various forms of reward that may be gained.

Tell them to decide on text together and that they should try to illustrate their leaflet or poster with drawings. Once the work is completed each small group should swap their poster or leaflet with another group and invite them to comment on its effectiveness and appeal.

(15 mins) Plenary

Discuss the motivation to work. Talk about why some people who win a lot of money still go on working when they no longer need to.

You might consider introducing the idea of people who work and make money through illegal means – the 'black' economy – but this could be a delicate subject in some communities where that kind of practice is very evident. Ask the children about aspects of the fairness and justice of this kind of work. Talk about the fact that the black economy is often based on criminal activities such as theft, burglary, drugs, and illicit buying and selling of goods.

Differentiation

The less able children will need help to prepare their leaflet or poster and may be aided by some suggested headings. Alternatively, invite them to draw their ideas of a rewarding job.

Encourage the more able children to research other ideas of what work might be like in the future.

Assessing learning outcomes

Can the children discuss different ideas of what constitutes work? Can they appreciate the benefits of work to the individual and society? Are the children able to express their views and opinions about the reasons why people choose to avoid regular work?

ICT opportunities
Use a graphics package on the computer to produce the leaflet or poster.

Follow-up activity
Invite people in various jobs to talk to the children on the subject of their motivation for work. The children could prepare a short interview schedule.

① hour How do we define the terms 'healthy' and 'unhealthy'?

Learning objectives
● Understand that people's health depends on the choices they are able to make.
● Appreciate that many people live in societies where their choices are limited.

Lesson organisation
Initial teacher-led, whole-class discussion; small-group activity; whole-class discussion; plenary.

Vocabulary
health
environment
beneficial
inequality
unhealthy
disease
medicines

ICT opportunities
Children could research the activities of charities such as Oxfam on the Internet (www.oxfam.org.uk).

Follow-up activity
Invite a speaker who has worked on charity projects for people in this country or abroad. The children could prepare questions about the perceived and actual impact that such work has on people's lives.

What you need and preparation
You will need facts about health in the developed and developing world supported by illustrative material of the type developed by Oxfam or Save the Children. Photocopiable pages 151 to 154 provide this. You will also need a large world map to locate the areas mentioned. The children will need reporting sheets and writing materials.

What to do

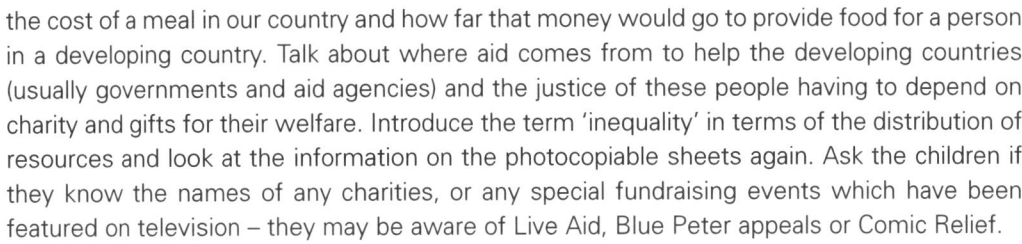

⏱20 mins Introduction
Introduce the subject of the 'healthy' and 'unhealthy' world. Explain that we all suffer poor health from time to time but, by comparison with those in the developing world, we have an extremely healthy environment and lifestyle.

Distribute copies of photocopiable page 151 to highlight the comparative use of resources such as food, water and the use of energy.

Explore some of the costs involved in helping to keep children healthy in some of the developing countries. Compare the cost of a meal in our country and how far that money would go to provide food for a person in a developing country. Talk about where aid comes from to help the developing countries (usually governments and aid agencies) and the justice of these people having to depend on charity and gifts for their welfare. Introduce the term 'inequality' in terms of the distribution of resources and look at the information on the photocopiable sheets again. Ask the children if they know the names of any charities, or any special fundraising events which have been featured on television – they may be aware of Live Aid, Blue Peter appeals or Comic Relief.

⏱25 mins Development
Divide the class into groups and give each group a copy of photocopiable pages 151–154. Explain that they should read the information comparing children in Cameroon and Germany, then try to visualise it and present it as a picture. Help the children to appreciate that a drawing can be a much more powerful way of getting ideas across. Tell them that photocopiable page 151 has an example of how to visualise an idea and may be of help to them.

⏱15 mins Plenary
Discuss special fundraising projects or campaigns and their value: *Do you think they do any lasting good or do they only have a temporary effect?* Ask the children if they have been involved in any such campaigns and what persuaded them to help.

Discuss with the children why some people choose to ignore these pleas for help and behave as though it has nothing to do with them.

Differentiation
The less able children will need help to visualise the ideas and should select just one or two.

More able children could visualise more of the information on the photocopiable sheets.

Assessing learning outcomes
Do the children appreciate that the world is a place of inequality? Are they able to appreciate that everyone has a responsibility to help alleviate suffering, even in a small way?

① Why do people break the laws of our society?

What you need and preparation
Collect a number of pictures of various criminal acts, such as burglary, physical injury or damage to property. Make some copies of photocopiable page 155, prepare reporting/rewording sheets for the children and provide writing materials.

What to do
⑳ Introduction
Ask the children why they think people break rules or laws. They may suggest that this is for personal gain, because they don't believe in them, or because they see other people doing the same thing. Discuss the statement that *people who break the law create an unfair society* and explain that it is unfair because they often take or damage something that is not rightly theirs. Mention the legend of Robin Hood – someone who is famous for robbing the rich to give to the poor. Point out that even this didn't make his acts of robbery right.

Now introduce the topic of crime among young people – children stealing, breaking into cars or damaging property. Suggest that these young criminals cannot have much respect for other people and their belongings if they can treat them in this way. Follow up this concept of respect – for the law, and for rules – and suggest that this lack of respect may lead to a dangerous lawless society. Hand out copies of photocopiable page 155 and encourage the children to discuss the issues it raises. *Do you think that people are dissuaded by the thought of being caught and punished or do they never consider this?* Talk to the children about the notion of bringing criminals face-to-face with the victim of their crimes: *Would this help to make amends? Is it a good idea? Is it fair?*

㉚ Development
Divide the class into small groups and explain that each group has to write and perform a short play or sketch based on the theme of the unfairness of crime.

Tell them that the choice and form of the storyline is theirs, that they can introduce as many characters (adults or children) into the story as they wish, and they can set the story in any type of location.

Encourage each group to begin by brainstorming a basic story or plot and then start to build the characters and the shape of the story.

Allow as much time as possible for the groups to work on their stories. Then either ask them to describe their sketches or plays to another group or, if time permits, perform them in another follow-up lesson.

Bring the class together to discuss what the writing (and performing) of the sketch meant and taught them. *What issues came up during the making of the sketch?*

Learning objectives
● Understand that people may exhibit lawful or unlawful behaviour.
● Develop notions of justice.

Lesson organisation
Initial teacher-led, whole-class discussion; small-group activity; whole-class discussion; plenary.

Vocabulary
law
order
disorder
unlawful
illegal
rights
punishment

10 mins **Plenary**

Encourage the groups to discuss their feelings towards people who break rules or laws: *Do you feel that it is unfair? Do these people seem to get an unfair advantage?* Discuss the view that *crime never pays*. If the children, or members of their families, have ever been victims of a criminal, how do they feel towards that person?

Ask the children how they feel about people receiving apparently light punishments for the crimes they have committed.

Differentiation

Provide the less able children with an outline structure of how the play could be written.

More able children could carry out research on the Internet to find statistics on a particular topic, such as child crime.

Assessing learning outcomes

Can the children link crime or unlawful behaviour with unfairness and inequality? Do they identify with the issue on a personal level?

Follow-up activity
A representative of the police may be prepared to talk to the children about crime and inequality and how the police perceive these to be interlinked.

1 hour What is equality of opportunity?

Learning objectives
● Learn that equality of opportunity, in terms of gender, is a major issue within our society.
● Appreciate that attitudes towards equal opportunities can be complex.

Lesson organisation
Initial teacher-led, whole-class discussion; paired and group activities; group discussion; plenary.

What you need and preparation

Make copies of photocopiable pages 156 and 157. Provide a wide selection of writing and colouring materials, including paper of different sizes, for the children to create leaflets and posters.

What to do

20 mins **Introduction**

Ask the children: *What do you think equal opportunities means – opportunities for what?* The children may suggest work or money though there are also likely to be children who are unaware that there are major inequalities in these areas! Continue to discuss equal opportunities in school. Do boys and girls feel they are treated equally? Read out some of the statistics from photocopiable page 157, which highlights examples of inequality, and ask the children for their reactions.

Discuss the reasons why such inequality has occurred – male domination of management roles for many years, the woman's role as housewife and mother, and so on.

Ask the children if they can think of any experiences they have had that demonstrate inequality still exists. They may talk about the jobs they see women doing and some children may even relate it to what happens at home. This is a delicate area so should be handled carefully and should not come as a prompt from the teacher.

Divide the class into pairs and give a copy of photocopiable page 156 to each pair. Suggest that inequality is often related to people's attitudes. Ask them to look at the pictures and write down the jobs they would expect women to be doing in these working environments.

At the end of this exercise ask the children to read out their statements and discuss the reasoning and justification for what they have written.

25 mins **Development**

Divide the class into groups, distribute copies of photocopiable page 157 and read the instructions together. Explain that statistics and opinions, while valuable, do not always get through to people. A visual representation may be more convincing getting a message across.

Vocabulary
equality
gender
prejudice
attitudes
discrimination
rights
employment

Invite the children, within their groups, to portray the facts and opinions in as creative a way as possible, perhaps as a poster, leaflet or brochure. Provide advice on how to go about this – brainstorm ideas, record them, discuss each one, decide on the two or three best ideas and then either work on a combination of the two or three or focus on the one they think is the best.

At the end of the activity, ask each group to explain the messages behind their literature. Ask whether they applied the principles of equal opportunities to their own discussion and development of the 'product'. *Are you sure that everyone's ideas were listened to? Are you sure that no one's idea was discriminated against other than because it 'didn't do the job'? Did everyone feel fully involved in the production of the 'product'?*

15 mins Plenary
Talk to the children about equality of opportunity in their own lives, in school, at home, playing with friends and in their leisure activities. What do they observe and what do they think and feel about situations in which they observe inequality?

Talk too about the strong negative feelings associated with inequality – not feeling part of things, frustration, anger, disappointment and resentment. Sometimes these negative feelings can be more passive, such as resignation and acceptance.

Differentiation
Offer the less able children more help with the leaflet. You may need to discuss one or two of the statistics with them to prompt ideas.

The more able children could represent a greater number of the ideas contained on the photocopiable sheet. They could include more text, and a greater variety of visuals.

Assessing learning outcomes
Do the children appreciate the different areas in which inequality often occurs? Can they discuss and evaluate the reasons why inequality exists? Are they able to relate any aspect of this topic to their own participation in the activity?

Follow-up activities
● Ask the headteacher to talk about the school's policy on equal opportunities.
● Develop a children's equal opportunities charter for the school. Produce the findings as a report.

What sort of future?

Helping children to feel positive and confident about the future is an important objective, which is not always easily achieved. There are many factors that can mitigate against the development of positive attitudes, yet there is also tremendous pressure on young people to be successful, and achieve the highest goals possible. From a very early age in school, the pressure to be successful is a constant part of children's learning.

Technology is already a major contributor to some of the rigid and dramatic successes of our society and will continue to be so in the future. Helping children to feel positive and confident about the role of technology in their lives is another important objective. While many children at this age embrace the excitement and appeal of technology, it is necessary to help them adopt a balanced attitude towards its role in their lives.

Attitudes towards work amongst children are worthy of investigation – many of them are excited and challenged by it, particularly those who see, on a day-to-day basis, the rewards it brings. For others there are no such positive feelings, rather there is uncertainty and even, in some cases, disillusionment. Children need to be helped to understand the broader concept of work as it might apply to their lives in the future. Looking at the ways in which the nature and pattern of work has changed over recent times may help to illustrate the enormous potential for change and development in the future.

Everyone values the place of leisure and entertainment in their lives and in the future opportunities for this will expand dramatically. Children will, in particular, be able to interact with, and shape, the nature of entertainment much more than ever before. The concept of global entertainment will expand, with new and exciting developments in communication technology. Already, however, we see the negative and very dangerous possibilities for the exploitation of children in this area and such issues have to be faced and discussed.

The future of schooling is an interesting and challenging subject for discussion. Changes will continue to affect the children as learners and, ultimately, as parents. Responding to those changes, including the increasing role of the family in the education process, is a vital part of our future society.

Finally, it is the changes to the individual – particularly to their knowledge, skills and attitudes – that will, more than anything, contribute to the nature and quality of their life and that of the community of which they are a part. The activities in this final section allow children to consider and contemplate these vital changes to their lives.

Unit: What sort of future?

Enquiry questions	Learning objectives	Teaching activities	Further teaching activities	Learning outcomes	Cross-curricular links
What sort of... technology? How have advancements in technology improved our society? In what ways do advances in technology come at a cost?	• Appreciate that developments in the technology of the future may be the responsibility of today's children. • Understand what makes a particular technological advancement notable.	Discuss technological advances. Choose and develop ideas for future advances in technology.	• Design the front page of a newspaper covering the announcement of their new technological breakthrough. • Hold a display of the class ideas and projects for parents and visitors. • Invent a new piece of school equipment to be used by pupils.	*Children:* • appreciate that technology is constantly advancing in areas such as science, technology and medicine • understand the need to develop new technology • discuss the feasibility of their idea	Technology: developing new forms of communication; investigating new technological achievements.
What sort of... work? How has the nature of work changed over the last 100 years? What forms will work take in the future?	• Understand that, in the future, work will take a variety of forms. • Appreciate that the nature of work has changed dramatically in the last hundred years.	Consider working patterns – past, present and future – in the local area. Prepare maps to show how this has changed.	• Research a job from the past and turn it into a job for the future. • Imagine a 'working week' in the future – how much time would be spent working and how much in leisure? Draw up a timetable.	• appreciate and describe the differences in work patterns across the three time periods • appreciate the advantages and disadvantages of work in the different periods • respond with a personal perspective to their own prospects of work	Geography: using maps
What sort of... leisure or entertainment? How have forms of leisure and entertainment changed in recent times and why? What forms will leisure take in the future?	• Understand how leisure and entertainment have changed over the last 100 years. • Recognise that leisure and entertainment will change in the future.	Consider local leisure and entertainment facilities and recent changes in home entertainment. Build models of future leisure sites.	• Design a creative new sport. • Devise the storyline and location for a major new film production. • Think of ideas for a company looking to develop new products for 'home entertainment'.	• appreciate how leisure and recreational pursuits have changed and will continue to change • identify with the needs of other groups for forms of leisure and recreation • appreciate that their projects might not be welcomed by everyone in the community	Technology: changes in entertainment. Art and Design: model-making.
What sort of... school? In what ways has the children's school changed in the time they have been there? What factors bring about changes in schools?	• Appreciate the extent to which education has changed since Victorian times. • Communicate ways in which learning may change in the future.	Study differences between modern and Victorian schools. Play a team game where players talk on the subject of a key educational term for a specified length of time.	• Imagine that, in 2002, schools will start advertising on radio and TV. Design your school's advertisement. • Draw up a timetable for 2010 when all pupils will divide their time between learning in school, at home, in a library or technology centre and in a local business – finding out about what it does.	• appreciate how changes occur in school • evaluate particular changes	History: education and the Victorians.
What sort of... me? What sort of person would I hope to be in the future? What kinds of things shape people's futures?	• Understand that our lives are shaped by other people and by ourselves. • Anticipate how their lives may develop in the future.	Prepare a personal profile. Identify a recent incident that has changed their lives and use this to play a game.	• The year is 2015. Apply for a job to join a team of people on a space station. What would you say in your application? Be creative. • Write your best friend's horoscope for 2005! • Plan a class reunion for 2010. What would you do, where would you hold it, how would you get in touch with everybody, and so on?	• reflect on people or events that have influenced and shaped their lives • visualise their lives in the future and describe how they feel about it • see how other people may play a part in their future.	Art and Design: drawing a self-portrait.

 # What sort of... technology?

Learning objectives
● Appreciate that developments in the technology of the future may be the responsibility of today's children.
● Understand what makes a particular technological advancement notable.

Lesson organisation
Initial teacher-led, whole-class discussion and small-group activity; paired activity and discussion; research task; whole-class discussion; plenary.

What you need and preparation

Copy and enlarge the pictures of technological advances from photocopiable page 158. You will also need copies of the photocopiable sheet for each group. You will need writing and drawing materials, card, and other materials for the children's drawings or for the construction of objects.

What to do

(25 mins) Introduction

Introduce the children to the idea of technological advancement. Ask them what notable achievements they think have been made in their lifetime, and encourage them to consider extended space travel, communication technology (such as satellites) and inventions to help people with disabilities. They may come up with other suggestions that will promote discussion, such as genetically modified food or cloning animals. Use the pictures from photocopiable page 158 to prompt their ideas. Ask the children to form small groups, give a copy of photocopiable page 158 to each group and ask them to rate these technological advances in terms of their impact on society.

Ask the children to form pairs and give them time to choose, think about and then describe one notable technological achievement so that the rest of the class can guess what it is. They should 'grade' the information they give so that it is quite difficult to begin with but gets easier as more information is given.

Discuss what makes a technological advancement notable. *Is it because it is unique, has a particular impact, or has benefits for a large number of people?* Ask the children: *Which technological advancement do you think has had the most impact on your life?* Suggest that they go home and put this question to their parents, friends or relations.

Collate these contributions when they come back to school and examine the results. Finish this part of the lesson by working around the class asking the children to complete the sentence: *The area of technological advancement that I would most like to have been part of would be...* (space exploration, medical advances, transport, technology, and so on). Conclude with the idea that not all so-called advancements have been for the good and that people have different opinions about the value of certain advancements, such as the mobile phone.

(20 mins) Development

Start with a whole-class discussion of what the future might hold for technology. If the children do not have ideas of their own prompt them with suggestions like using more robotics, or advancements in automotive technology.

Ask the children to pair up and discuss what kind of technological advancement they would like to work on in the future. Between them they should choose one item or idea they would wish to develop.

After their initial discussion, tell the pairs that they may work on their own chosen project. Remind them that the object should make a significant contribution to people's lives (or a particular group of people). Invite the children to draw and/or describe the object. If time, and other resources, permit, they might build a model of the object too. They should also write a short explanation of how and why they had the idea and why they think it would make a valuable contribution to people's lives.

Encourage the children to share their ideas with at least two other pairs in the class so that they receive some feedback. This should allow them to develop the idea more fully. Remind

Vocabulary
technology
advancement
progress
benefit
feasibility
desirability

the children that they also need to think about the feasibility of their ideas: *How realistic is it that one day something like the object you've drawn could exist?* Make a class display of all the work and put up a comments sheet to allow the children to say what they think of the different ideas.

15 mins Plenary

Discuss the fact that we almost take technology for granted. Tell the children that today a mobile phone is just a normal everyday feature, but ten years ago it was not. Nobody thinks twice about the fact that we can watch things happening 'live' all over the world, but television is a fairly recent invention too.

Encourage the class to talk about their projects: *How hard was it to think of something innovative or unique?* Ask the children to talk about the origins of their ideas: *What prompted you to think of this project? Did you know someone who would benefit from the item?* Ask the children to consider how they think their idea would be received by other people.

Differentiation

Offer the less able children support by suggesting some areas they might like to consider such as: objects for particular groups of people; objects that make people's work easier or their time at home more comfortable.

The more able children should provide extra detail on their objects, and present a feasibility study, along with some estimates.

Assessing learning outcomes

Do the children appreciate that technology is constantly advancing in areas such as science, technology and medicine? Can they understand the need to develop new technology? Can they discuss the feasibility of their idea?

1 hour What sort of... work?

What you need and preparation

Collect some drawings of people doing a range of jobs from approximately a hundred years ago. You will also need drawing and writing materials, including sheets of card and access to a board or flipchart.

Prepare two large maps of your local area – one to represent the area now and one to represent it a hundred years ago. You will need a copy of each map for each group. Find some books on local history – with particular reference to people's occupations – and an encyclopaedia or historical reference book that illustrates jobs from an earlier century.

What to do

15 mins Introduction

Ask the children to imagine that they were living a hundred years ago. *What jobs do you think you would have been doing then? Do you think you would be working on the land, in a mine or in a factory?* Display the pictures you have collected to help start the discussion. Make a list of the children's suggestions on the board. Ask, and discuss, their opinions on whether they think working life was harder then than it is today.

Talk about the types of jobs – many would have involved making things or working on the land. The children could work in small groups to represent all these different jobs on the map of their town or village – marking the different occupations people had and where they worked.

What sort of
future?

Vocabulary
work
employment
jobs
occupation
manufacturing
service sector
factory
office
skills

The map should be entitled: *Work – a hundred years ago*. Distribute the books you collected to help the children with the task.

Development
30 mins Tell the children that they are going to work, in pairs, on a map, or time chart, entitled: *Work – as it is now*. Encourage them to think of all the differences between work a hundred years ago and now, and to find ways of representing these ideas on the map or time chart. They are likely to identify that there is less work outdoors, more work in the service sector, less work in manufacturing, longer journeys to work, less individual work and more work in groups, different hours of work and more time for leisure.

Once these maps or charts have been completed ask the children, in the same pairs, to discuss what work will be like in a hundred years from now. You may need to ask some questions to get them started: *Where do you think most people will be working – in offices, at home, or in factories? What sorts of jobs will they have? What hours will they work? When will they start and finish? What sort of technology will be available to help them?* (robotics, more satellite communication, more advanced microcomputers).

Plenary
15 mins Bring the children together to talk about their ideas of work now and in the future: *Do you regard working as very important? Do you look forward to the idea of working? What kind of place would you like to work in? What kind of work would you like to do? Would you like to work for yourself?*

Encourage the children to discuss the advantages and disadvantages of work in the three different time settings. If a person made something a hundred years ago, they saw it through from the beginning to the end. That is now less likely to be true. Many people today work for large international companies, not just a local business as people would have done a hundred years ago. Many more people now have to travel abroad with their work than a hundred years ago and this amount of travel may increase in the future. 150 years ago people would know (even if they hadn't met them) the owner of the company – probably an individual or a family.

Follow-up activity
Encourage the children to talk to other people who have had experience of different work patterns and locations. They may be able to add detail and enhance the children's appreciation of the changing patterns of work.

Differentiation
Provide outlines and key words to help the less able children with the maps. You could also prepare some questions for this group to answer on the map.

The more able children could be offered more questions or clues to help them identify how such patterns of work might have come about.

Assessing learning outcomes
Can the children appreciate and describe the differences in work patterns across the three time periods? Do they appreciate the advantages and disadvantages of work in the different periods? Do the children respond with a personal perspective to their own prospects of work?

① What sort of… leisure or entertainment?

What you need and preparation

Prepare a large map of your local town or village for each group and collect some old photographs from the area depicting leisure and recreational activities. You will also need writing and drawing materials, card, adhesive and adhesive tape, and other materials to make models of small buildings. You will need access to a board or flipchart.

What to do

⑳ Introduction

Introduce the terms leisure and entertainment by talking to the children about their local environment, encouraging them to think about all the different forms of leisure and entertainment available to people, such as the cinema, a bingo hall, a leisure centre, or the park. Ask the children if they can work out a timeline for these: *Which are the oldest, which are the newest? Do you know of any leisure facilities which have ceased to exist?*

Write the children's suggestions on the board. Potentially, this could be a long list, and may need some form of classification to guide the discussion. Encourage the children to classify them in terms of 'recent', 'quite old' and 'very old'.

Change the focus of the discussion to how leisure and entertainment in the home have changed. Ask the children to think about the leisure activities that were available a hundred years ago and to make a comparison between leisure then and now.

Encourage them to think about the things that have brought about major changes in leisure and entertainment in the home – the introduction of television, video, the Internet, and so on. Discuss the advantages and disadvantages of these changes.

㉚ Development

Divide the class into small groups and give each group one of the maps of their local area and the materials to make model buildings (see What you need and preparation).

Ask them to build models to represent their ideas of the leisure 'sites' or 'activities' that will be available in their area a hundred years from now. Encourage them to be as imaginative as possible and suggest that technology, multimedia and virtual reality will play a big part. Remind them that they need to consider the needs of different sectors of the community – not just young people.

Give each group time to present their project to the class (you will probably need to allow another session for this) and invite the other groups to give feedback on the idea. Talk about any potential local opposition to the idea. *How would you respond to that?*

Once the children have done their presentations put their work on display and attach a comments sheet for other children to offer further ideas or opinions.

⑩ Plenary

Bring the class together to discuss their understanding of leisure and entertainment. *Was your facility just a fun, pleasurable, recreational item or could it offer other types and forms of leisure? Can something be educational and entertainment at the same time?*

Talk to the children about the fact that people will probably have more leisure time in a hundred years than they have now. *How would this change your ideas?* Suggest that people might be able to travel further for entertainment; that they might be able to experience and join in some forms of external entertainment without leaving their own homes; and that entertainment generally might be more global.

Learning objectives
● Understand how leisure and entertainment have changed over the last hundred years.
● Recognise that leisure and entertainment will change in the future.

Lesson organisation
Initial teacher-led, whole-class discussion; group activity; project work; whole-class discussion of projects; plenary.

Vocabulary
leisure
recreation
entertainment
relaxation
interests
hobbies

Differentiation

Help the less able children with the planning exercise – offer some suggestions of forms of leisure to consider, such as a virtual reality adventure playground.

The more able children could be challenged to consider other types of leisure, ones that are not just for fun.

Assessing learning outcomes

Do the children appreciate how leisure and recreational pursuits have changed and will continue to change? Can they identify with the needs of other groups for forms of leisure and recreation? Do they appreciate that their projects might not be welcomed by everyone in the community?

Follow-up activities
● Formulate a proposal to the local council outlining the ideas, and their appeal, as well as the advantages to the economy of the area.
● Design a poster advertising a selected site or activity, describing it in some detail so that it will appeal to a particular age group.

What sort of... school?

What you need and preparation

Make a pack of 'school cards' for each group of children with one of the following words on each of them: *place*, *time*, *subjects*, *resources*, *games*, *uniform*, *special events* and *teachers*. If you think of other relevant words you could add these too.

If possible, collect some photographs of the school and the surrounding area from the past. Make a copy of photocopiable page 159 for each group. You will also need writing materials, an account or description of a Victorian classroom, (novels by Charles Dickens will provide these) and watches with second hands, or other timing devices.

Learning objectives
● Appreciate the extent to which education has changed since Victorian times.
● Communicate ways in which learning may change in the future.

Lesson organisation
Initial teacher-led, whole-class discussion; small-group activity; group game; whole-class discussion; plenary.

Vocabulary
classroom
learning
knowledge
skills
technology
resources

What to do

20 mins Introduction

Talk to the children about change and how it affects them. *Have there been any changes to the school since you joined it?* Use the photographs to describe the physical changes that have taken place over a longer period of time – *it's bigger, smarter, it is now surrounded by houses*. You could also talk about changes which have taken place internally. Move on to discuss non-physical changes, such as what is taught or rules and regulations. Explore with the children some of the reasons why these changes have occurred.

Divide the class into small groups. Give each group a copy of the photocopiable sheet and ask them to study all the differences (physical and organisational) between the modern and the Victorian classroom.

Bring the class back together and discuss their observations. Read an account or description of a Victorian classroom to develop the idea of change. Then go around the class and ask the children to finish the sentence: *If I could change one thing in the school for the future it would be....* Devise a way of giving these ideas some feedback – let the other children provide a 'clapometer' verdict to show the strength of agreement.

(25 mins) Development

Divide the class into teams of four and pair up two teams. Give each team a pack of the school cards with the key words. (You can reproduce any number of cards so that key words appear more than once.) Explain that they are going to play a game, as follows.

The two packs are placed face down in front of each team and individual members of the teams take turns to pick up a card. That individual then has a choice – he or she can choose to speak for 20 seconds on as many changes related to that word as possible, as it applies to the school of the future. If they are successful, they earn 100 points for their team. If they hesitate, or run out of things to say, they lose 50 points for their team.

Alternatively, they can choose not to speak on the topic and give the card to their opponents, who have to accept the speaking challenge. If they fail to achieve the 20-second presentation, 50 points are awarded to the team who gave the card to them. If, however, they are successful (without hesitation or stops) they gain 200 points for their own team. Decide, in advance, on the time limit and provide some means of keeping time and the score.

(15 mins) Plenary

Discuss with the children the advantages and disadvantages of change. Ask them to give examples of changes, both good and bad, which have been made in school. Explore the idea of how changes come about. It may be because of dissatisfaction, protest, complaints, new suggestions or new experiences from other schools, and so on.

Differentiation

The less able children may not be able to manage a 20-second presentation but the more able children should certainly be able to fill that time. Adjust the timing and scoring systems for different abilities.

Assessing learning outcomes

Do the children appreciate how changes occur in school? Are they able to evaluate particular changes?

ICT opportunities
Carry out research on schools from the Victorian era on the Internet.

Follow-up activity
Design a school of the future by completing a plan and sketches.

(1 hour) What sort of... me?

What you need and preparation

Make a copy of photocopiable page 160 for each child in the class. Provide writing and drawing materials and scissors.

What to do

(25 mins) Introduction

Suggest to the children that, although we cannot predict the future, we can do things that help to shape our future. Point out that we are all acquiring knowledge, skills and attitudes, and developing qualities that will help us to achieve things in the future.

Discuss the idea that, although it is not their choice whether they go to school or not, they do have a choice as to how hard they work, how successful they are and therefore, in part, what sort of future they will have. Tell them that while they are at school, as well as acquiring new knowledge and new skills, they develop attitudes, values and opinions which begin to shape them as people.

Divide the children into pairs and give each child a copy of photocopiable page 160. Ask them to look at the sheets, discuss them, draw a picture of themselves and then cut out the

Learning objectives
● Understand that our lives are shaped by other people and by ourselves.
● Anticipate how their lives may develop in the future.

Lesson organisation
Initial teacher-led, whole-class discussion; paired activity and discussion; group activity and discussion; plenary.

What sort of future?

Vocabulary
ambition
priority
progression
advancement

word and phrases they feel are of value in shaping them as people. They should then complete their personal profile by sticking the pieces they have cut out around their self-portrait. Each pair should then compare their profiles with those of two other children.

Ask the children to publish their profiles by displaying them on the classroom wall and inviting other children to comment on them.

(20 mins) Development

Introduce the idea that our lives are shaped by the people we meet, and the events we encounter, and that most of this is beyond our control. At school the children meet new teachers and pupils. Outside school the arrival of new friends and neighbours may change the way they think and behave.

Encourage the children to think back over the last year and identify one incident that in some way (small or large) changed their lives. This might be meeting someone, a happy or sad event, a journey or a success. Ask a few of the children to talk about their incident and explain how they think it has changed them.

Divide the class into groups and challenge them to turn the above discussion into a game. This game should consist of a set of cards marked, *place, person, event*. All the children should contribute one personal story from their discussion to one of the three sets of *place, person, event*. These stories are then made into a pack of playing cards for each of the three sets. The children take it in turns to choose from one of the three sets. They have to decide on a scale of 1–10 how important the story was to the person to whom it happened. They check their rating with the person who wrote it. If they get it exactly right they score 10 points, if within 3, they score 5 points. The game carries on around the group and the winner is the person with the most points.

(15 mins) Plenary

Discuss with the children how they view the future: *Are you excited by the future? Do you give it any thought? Do you ever worry about it?* Invite them to give examples of their thoughts and feelings.

Talk about planning for the future: *Do you plan things for tomorrow, or next week, or do you just let things happen? Do you think there is any point making plans?*

Ask them if they think about the future beyond school: *What does the future look like? Could you begin to describe it? What do you hope it will look like? Do you think of the future in terms of yourself only or do you think about how other people will feature as part of it?*

Differentiation

Give the less able children support with the photocopiable sheet by offering prompts, such as: *What have you learned? What do you think you are good at? What sort of person do you think you are?*

Challenge the more able children to add other elements to the game.

Assessing learning outcomes

Can the children reflect on people or events that have influenced and shaped their lives? Are they able to visualise their lives in the future and describe how they feel about it? Can they see how other people would play a part in their future?

Follow-up activity
Encourage the children to play the game with their parents, friends or relations. They could find out how they view the future, as well as asking them to think back to critical moments that they feel shaped their lives.

Name _____   Date _____

Team goals

Name of the team:

We think that this team's goals would be

Goal A: _____ because _____

Goal B: _____ because _____

Goal C: _____ because _____

Goal D: _____ because _____

For the team's supporters/clients, the two most important goals would be:

_____

_____

For the team's manager/leader, the two most important goals would be:

_____

_____

Now write two sentences to complete the statement below.
To achieve these goals, the team would have to:

_____

_____

PHOTOCOPIABLE

BUILDING HEALTHY RELATIONSHIPS: Building a team
What is a team? Page 8

Name _____ Date _____

Planning sheet

These are the facilities we thought of for the leisure centre:

These are the six facilities we chose:

1.

2.

3.

4.

5.

6.

People cards

PHOTOCOPIABLE

BUILDING HEALTHY RELATIONSHIPS: **Building a team**
How do teams deal with difficult individuals? Page 9

Name _____ Date _____

Strengths and weaknesses

Strengths	Weaknesses
Confident	Can't stand failure in others
Responsible	Avoids taking the lead
Reliable	Cannot be depended upon
Loyal	Does not support friends when asked
Honest	Will lie if necessary
Consistent	Tends to have changes of mind when
Patient	it suits
Calm	Gets very irritated
	Becomes bad tempered

We think this person would be:

Strengths	Weaknesses

Name _____   Date _____

I think... what do you think?

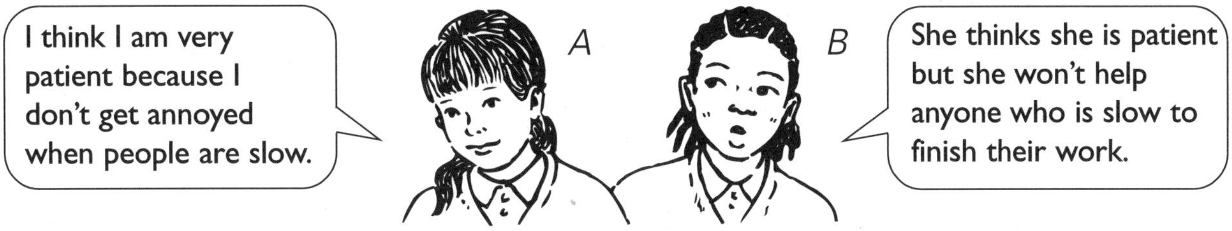

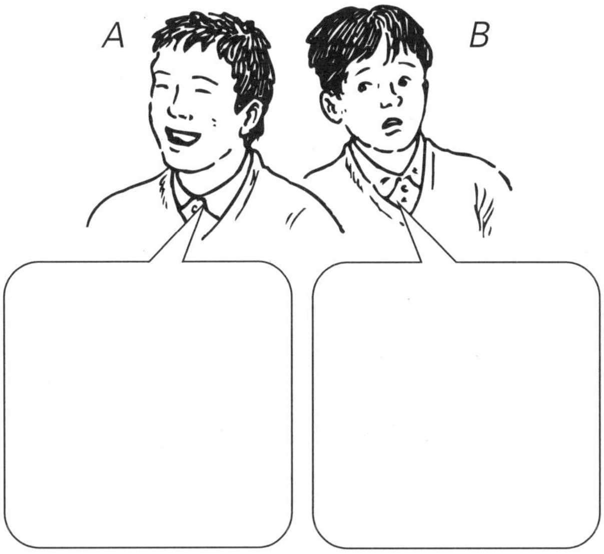

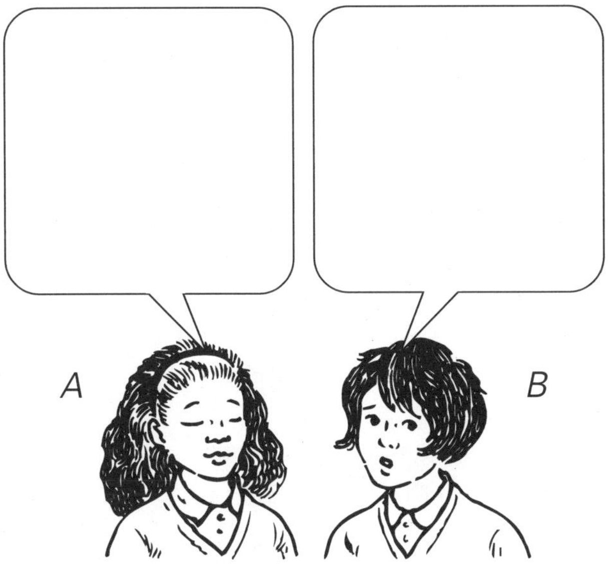

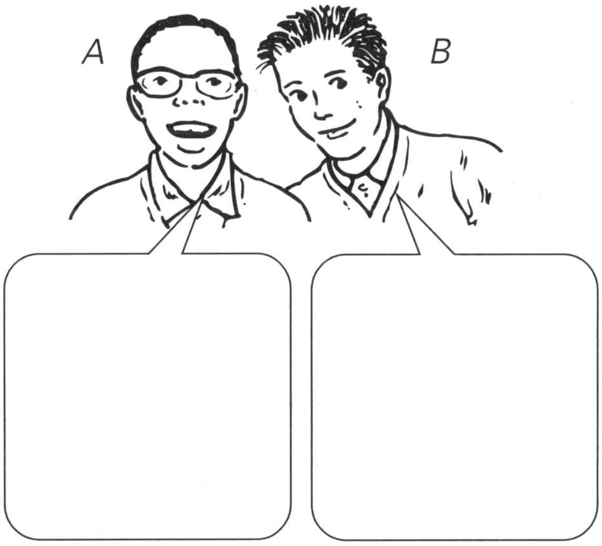

> I think I am very patient because I don't get annoyed when people are slow.

> She thinks she is patient but she won't help anyone who is slow to finish their work.

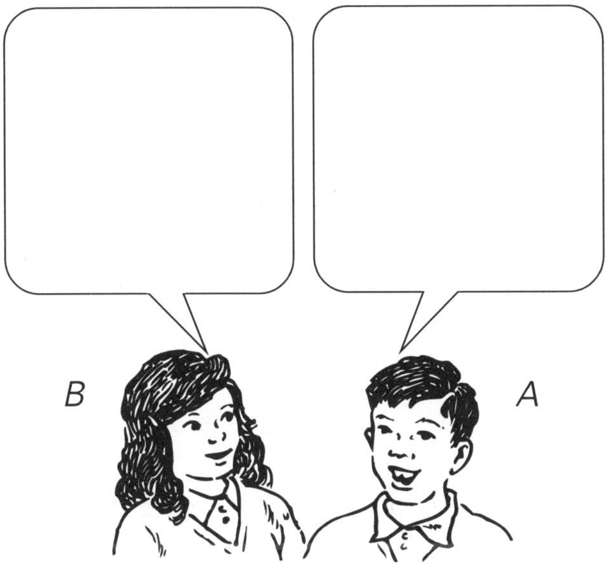

Write a speech bubble for each person in this picture.
The speech bubble for A describes what that individual thinks of him or herself.
The speech bubble for B describes what B thinks of A's description. One example has been done for you.

PHOTOCOPIABLE

BUILDING HEALTHY RELATIONSHIPS: Building a team
What makes a team successful? Page 10

Name _____   Date _____

Holiday planning contract

In order to have a successful holiday, we need the following information and skills:

This information or these skills are important to the success of the holiday because:

We think you _____ have this knowledge or skill because we know that you can:

We would like you to prepare the information/do this task for us.
We think that it will take you:

Signed: _____

Name _____   Date _____

My leadership ambition

Name: _____

I would like to lead a team of people to:

because:

I think I would be a good leader because:

I know…

I'm good at…

I'm the sort of person who is…

I would like these people in my team because:

Name: Reason:

Name: Reason:

Name: Reason:

PHOTOCOPIABLE

BUILDING HEALTHY RELATIONSHIPS: Building a team
What kinds of problems do teams encounter? Page 13

Name _____ Date _____

Conflict

These people could be arguing because

_____

_____

I suggest they could solve their differences by

_____

_____

These people could be arguing because

_____

_____

I suggest they could solve their differences by

_____

_____

These people could be arguing because

_____

_____

I suggest they could solve their differences by

_____

_____

These people could be arguing because

_____

_____

I suggest they could solve their differences by

_____

_____

Name _____   Date _____

Our community groups

In your village, town or city, there will be many groups of people – different nationalities, different ages, different interest groups, different types of jobs. These groups will often be linked together in some way.

Use the circles to represent who the groups are and add a word or phrase to explain each link.

PHOTOCOPIABLE

BUILDING HEALTHY RELATIONSHIPS: Building a nation
What types of groupings exist within a nation? Page 18

Name _____   Date _____

Map of the British Isles

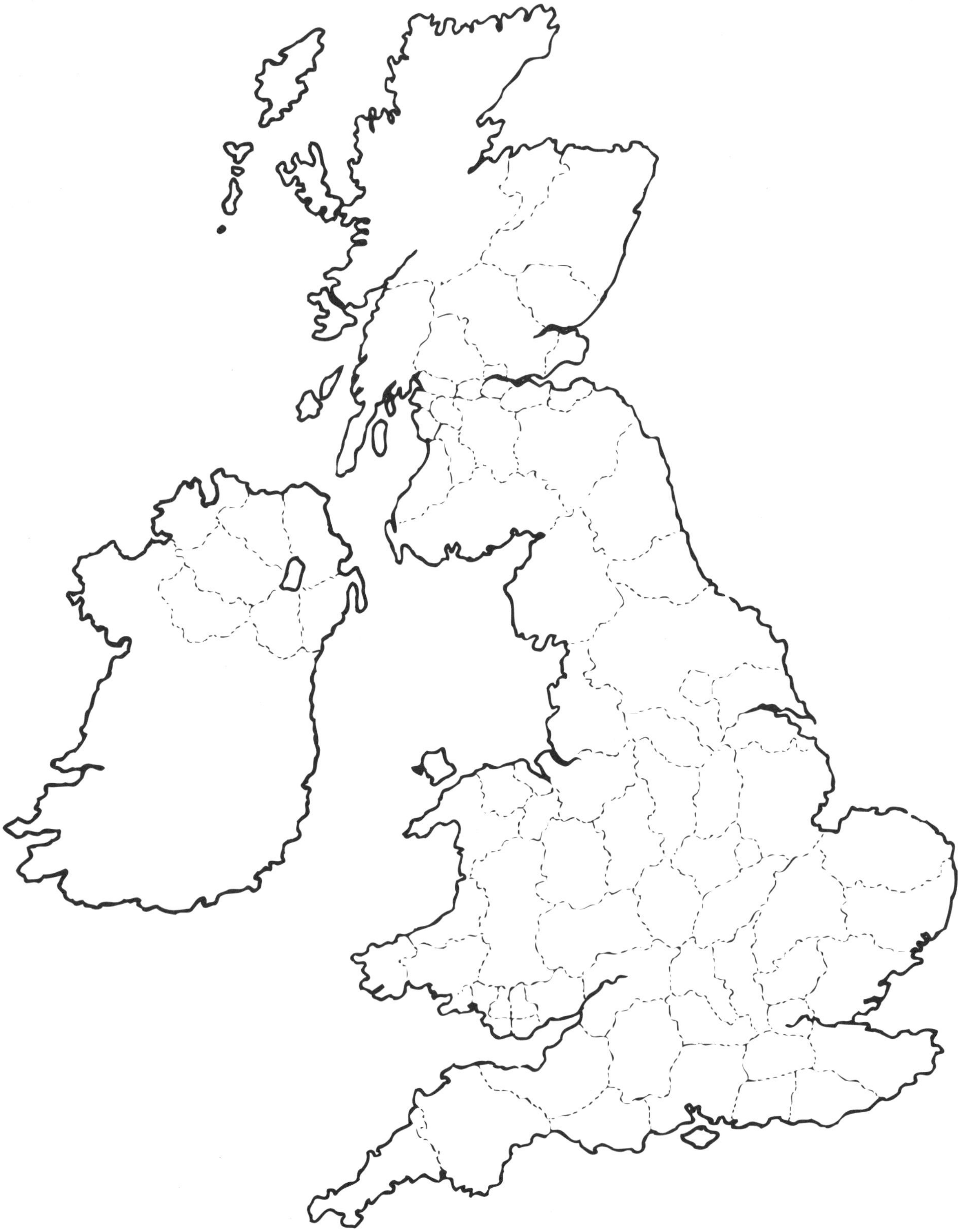

The image of our town

This is a drawing of a street which might be in your town.
Decide whether it gives a good or bad image of the town, then write down what you think on the back of the sheet.
Look for the evidence in the picture.
Discuss your thoughts with a partner.

A healthy society?

These are pictures of scenes that some people see every day of their lives.
They are indicators that we live in an 'unhealthy' society.
Discuss what a visitor to our country would think about these places.

PHOTOCOPIABLE

Name _____   Date _____

Government debate

Observation sheet

This is your checklist of how well people debated the law.
Write the rules your teacher drew up at the start of the lesson on both sides
– for Government and Opposition. Mark with an X each time you think a rule
was broken.

Government	**Opposition**
Rule:	Rule:
Rule:	Rule:
Rule:	Rule:
Rule:	Rule:

Name _____   Date _____

High risk – low risk?

Look at these pictures and decide if there is a 'risk' attached to what the person is doing. Assess (on a scale of 1–10) how high that risk is.

Name _____   Date _____

What do you say?

Look at this picture and complete the speech bubble for each child.
One is trying to persuade the other to do something. The second child's
response should give reasons for not behaving in that way.

PHOTOCOPIABLE

BUILDING HEALTHY BODIES: A healthy choice
How are people affected by advertising? Page 31

Name _____ Date _____

An advertisement for health?

Use the following questions to review an advertisement for a product related to healthy living.

1. What is the message(s) contained within the advertisement?

2. Who is the advertisement aimed at?

3. Does it use: ☐ text?   ☐ images?   ☐ sound?

4. Which of these, do you think, were the most effective?

5. Did the advertisement give you **information** about the product as well as trying to persuade you to buy it?

6. Did you find the advertisement:

☐ appealing ☐ entertaining ☐ persuasive ☐ off-putting ☐ misleading?

Give your reasons:

7. If you had the opportunity to change the advertisement in any way, what would you do to it?

8. Are there any conflicting 'messages' in this advertisement? (Perhaps related to healthy living, taking care of our bodies, behaving sensibly and responsibly or thinking about other people's feelings?)

Road safety

You might like to illustrate some of these pieces of road safety information on your poster or leaflet.

- About 9000 children are killed or injured in road accidents every year.
- Many accidents, however, are not reported – the figure could be nearer to 90 000.
- Boys are more likely to be killed or injured than girls, both as pedestrians and as cyclists.
- Accidents outside school gates are rare – most child accidents occur near to where children live.
- Children below the age of 11 are more likely to be in an accident on a minor road than on a main road.
- Nearly one third of 8–11 year old pedestrian accidents occur when children are crossing between parked cars.
- Children between 8–11 pose very little threat to other road users.

These statistics are taken from the British Institute of Traffic Education Research.

BUILDING HEALTHY BODIES: **Healthy exercise**

PHOTOCOPIABLE   In what ways is 'time' a resource? Page 37

Name _____   Date _____

How I spend my day

Use this clock to record how your day, between 8am and 8pm, is divided between such things as eating, exercising, relaxing and working (including school). Record the names of the activities in the middle section, as shown. Compare your clock with someone else's. Discuss whether the balance or proportion of the different activities is about right.

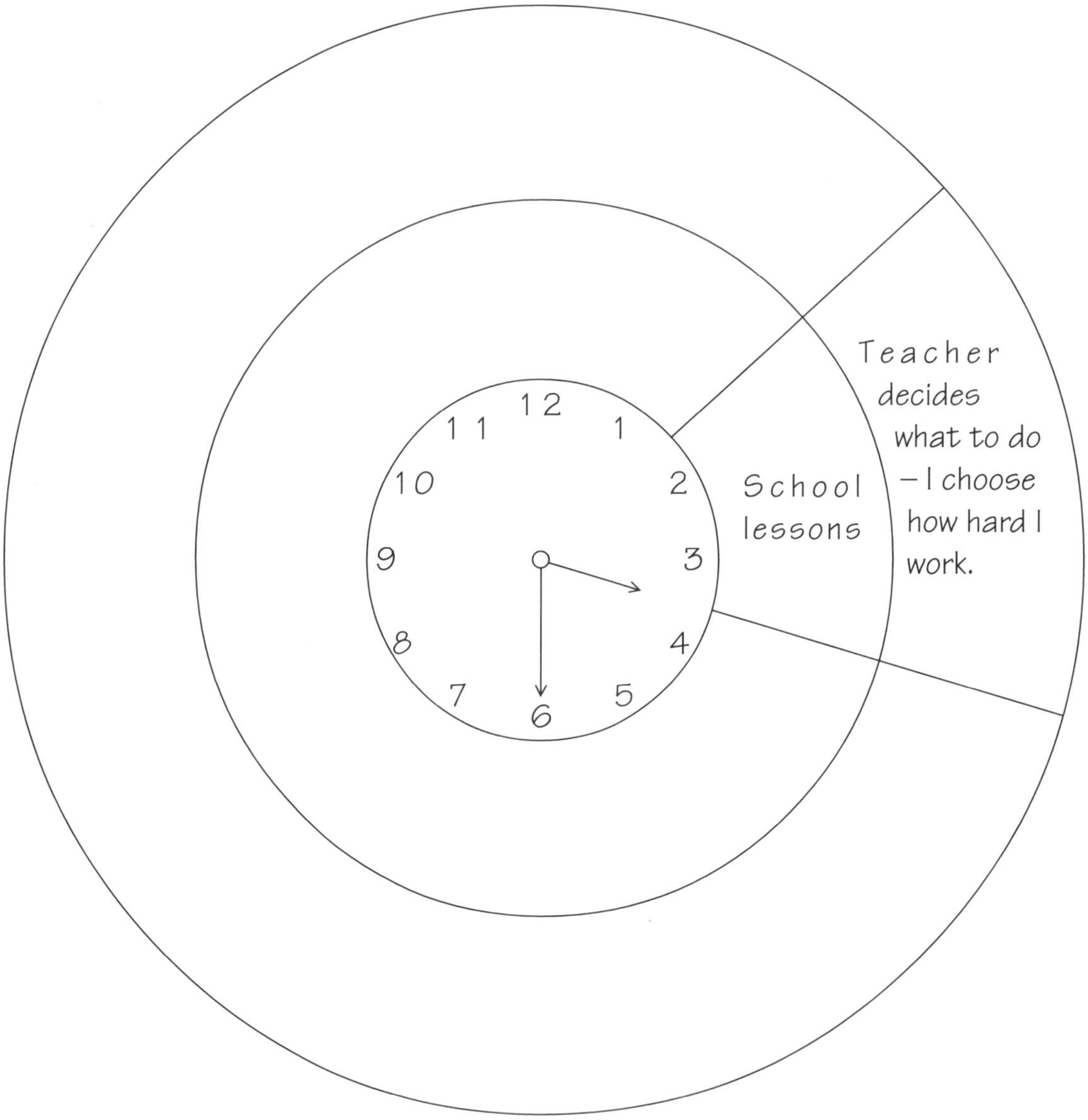

School lessons

Teacher decides what to do – I choose how hard I work.

In the outermost ring of the 'clock', indicate whether the activity is determined by you or by someone else. Again, one example have been done for you. What does this information show about who decides how you spend your day?

BUILDING HEALTHY BODIES: **Healthy exercise**

In what ways is 'time' a resource? Page 37

PHOTOCOPIABLE

Name _____   Date _____

Diary page

Use this diary page to record how much of your week was spent doing 'healthy things'.

	Activity	Effect
Monday		
Tuesday		
Wednesday		
Thursday		
Friday		
Saturday		
Sunday		

PHOTOCOPIABLE

BUILDING HEALTHY BODIES: **Healthy exercise**
Do we need to exercise our minds? Page 39

Name _____   Date _____

Is it exercise?

These drawings show people doing different activities – are they all exercising?

BUILDING HEALTHY BODIES: Healthy exercise
What are costs and benefits? Page 40

PHOTOCOPIABLE

Costs and benefits

Look at the pictures on this sheet. They show children doing certain tasks. For each one work out the 'costs' (disadvantages) and 'benefits' (advantages) of that activity. Try to think of as many costs and benefits as you can and record these on the recording sheet.

1

2

3

4

PHOTOCOPIABLE

BUILDING HEALTHY BODIES: Healthy exercise
What are costs and benefits? Page 40

Name _____ Date _____

Recording costs and benefits

Record the costs and benefits of each activity in the first two columns. Assess the level of the cost or benefit in the third column and make your personal response in the last column.

	Costs	Benefits	How high or low (on a scale of 0–10) are the costs and benefits?	Would I regard the costs as outweighing the benefits or vice versa?
Picture 1				
Picture 2				
Picture 3				
Picture 4				

City scene

Country scene

Name _____   Date _____

Feelings map

Shade in the sectors with different colours and provide a key to illustrate the strength of your 'feelings' for these 'environments'.

Beyond my country

My country

My village/town/city

My street

My home

My area

Name _____   Date _____

Environment recording sheet

Fill in this sheet to show your feelings about caring for a particular environment. Use it to record your discussion.

This is an environment we should care a lot about because…

This is an environment we should care a little for, because…

We had a difference of opinion on…

We were totally agreed on…

Name _____   Date _____

Storyboard

Write the storyline for this storyboard and complete the last two boxes with pictures and the storyline.

1 	**2** 
Middle-aged man walking along the street.	Youths playing in street – throwing tins and bottles.
3 	**4** 
Man 'confronts' youths.	Youths 'turn on' man.
5	**6**

BUILDING HEALTHY ENVIRONMENTS: *Your life – your choice*
Do we affect our environment? Page 48

PHOTOCOPIABLE

Choice cards

I would not do anything about someone who I saw…	I would stop behaving in a certain way if…
I would do something about someone who I saw…	I would not stop behaving in a certain way unless…
I would try to find someone to tell if I saw…	I would try to persuade other people to behave as I did by…

Everyday people and places

BUILDING HEALTHY ENVIRONMENTS: Your life – your choice

PHOTOCOPIABLE   How healthy is our community? Page 52

Town centre map

LIBRARY

HOUSING ESTATE

CHURCH

GARAGE

THEATRE

FOOTBALL GROUND

SUPER-MARKET

HOTEL

CINEMA

OFFICE BLOCK

TOY FACTORY

GOLF COURSE

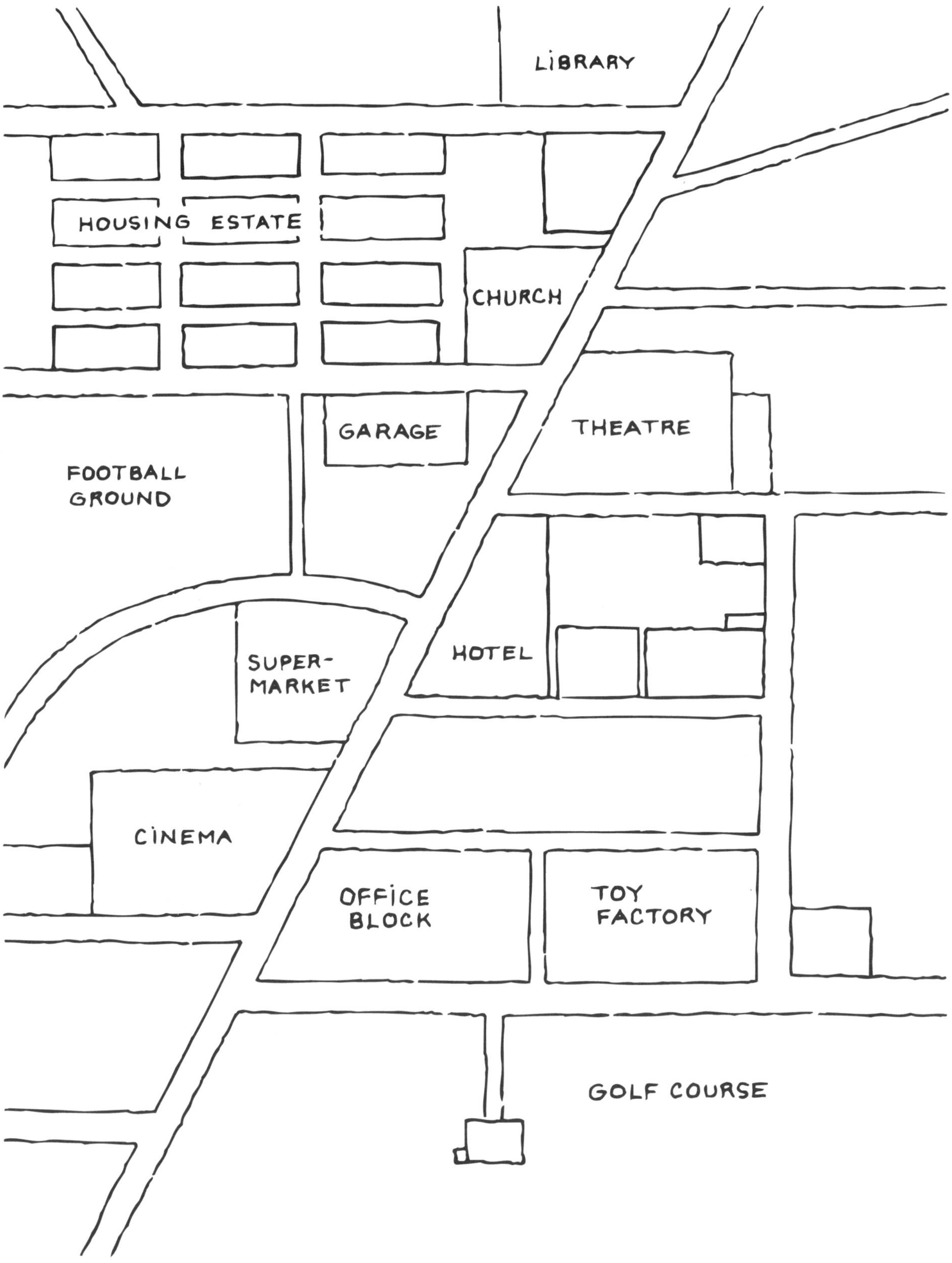

Name _____   Date _____

Action plan

Place or area selected (include a drawing)

Nature of the problem

Our recommended strategy for improvement

Reasons for the above

Ways of measuring its success

BUILDING HEALTHY ENVIRONMENTS: **Pollution – who's to blame?**

PHOTOCOPIABLE   Who shares the responsibility for pollution in our society? Page 57

Name _____   Date _____

Pollution quiz

Add some more questions, then challenge another group to answer your quiz.

1 Pollution is: a type of custard a pain in the back something which makes where we live untidy or unpleasant.	**6**
2 Exhaust pollution is caused by: cows birds cars.	**7**
3 Emission describes: a dangerous task a pop group what comes out of cars or factories.	**8**
4 Greenhouse gases are: gases used to grow tomatoes gases used to heat a greenhouse gases produced in the atmosphere.	**9**
5 Ozone is: a hairspray a type of fuel for cars a layer in our atmosphere.	**10**

PHOTOCOPIABLE

Name _____   Date _____

Land pollution

PHOTOCOPIABLE

BUILDING HEALTHY ENVIRONMENTS: Pollution – who's to blame?
What forms of air pollution affect the quality of our lives? Page 60

MARLTON GAZETTE

COUNCIL PURGE ON AIR POLLUTION

Marlton Council is determined that air pollution is going to be a thing of the past in their area! At a recent Council meeting the Environmental Sub Committee put forward its plans to clean up the Marlton air. The chairman of the committee said, "The time has come to stop playing games, pretending everything is OK. If people don't like what we're proposing then I'm sorry, but the health of everyone is our priority."

Among the measures the Council is proposing are:

- All restaurants will be no-smoking.
- All shops and offices will be no-smoking.
- All public transport will be no-smoking.
- The burning of garden rubbish by residents will be banned.
- The town centre will become a traffic-free precinct.
- Vehicle emissions will be thoroughly checked.
- Factories will be inspected annually for levels of emission.

The council are expecting some opposition to their proposals, but say they are prepared to defend them.

BUILDING HEALTHY ENVIRONMENTS: Pollution – who's to blame?
What are the major sources of water pollution? Page 61
PHOTOCOPIABLE

Map of Wexton

GOLF COURSE

HOUSING ESTATE

WEXTON FARM

RESIDENTIAL CARAVAN PARK

FACTORY SITE

PRODUCES UPHOLSTERY FOR CARS

PUB

SHOPS

SHOPS

LIBRARY

CINEMA

SHOPS

SHOPS

FISHERMAN'S SOCIAL CLUB

TOWN PARK

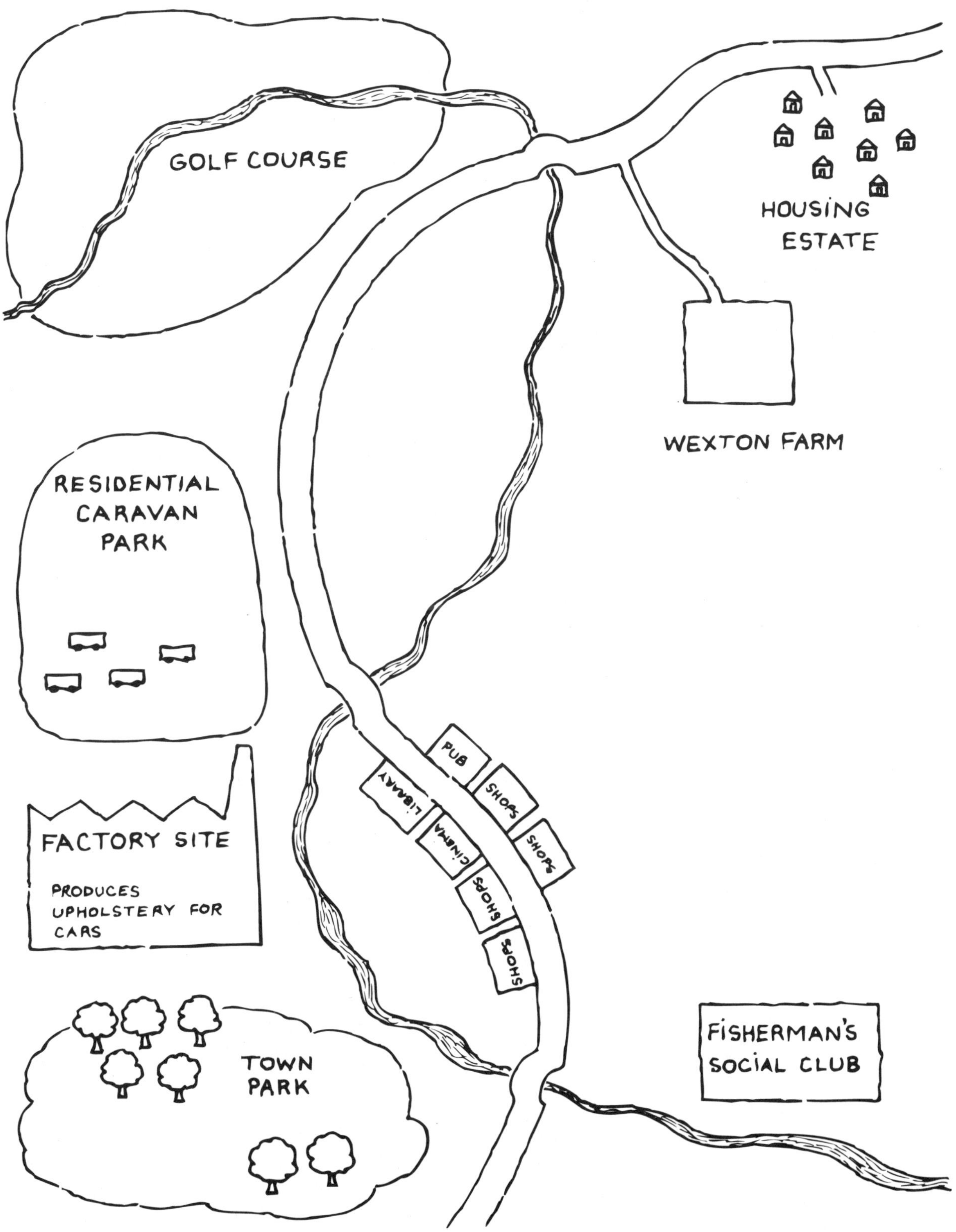

PHOTOCOPIABLE

BUILDING HEALTHY ENVIRONMENTS: Pollution – who's to blame?
Pollution – a worldwide problem? Page 62

Pollution diagrams

Diagram of air pollution

Damage to humans	Sulphur dioxide, oxides of hydrocarbons	Acid rain

Air pollution

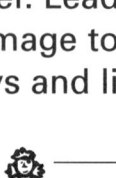

Respiratory diseases, increased risk of cancer. Lead – damage to kidneys and liver

Carbon monoxide, hydrocarbons, heavy metals, dust, organic compounds, soot

Damage to buildings and trees

Sources of acid rain: Norway

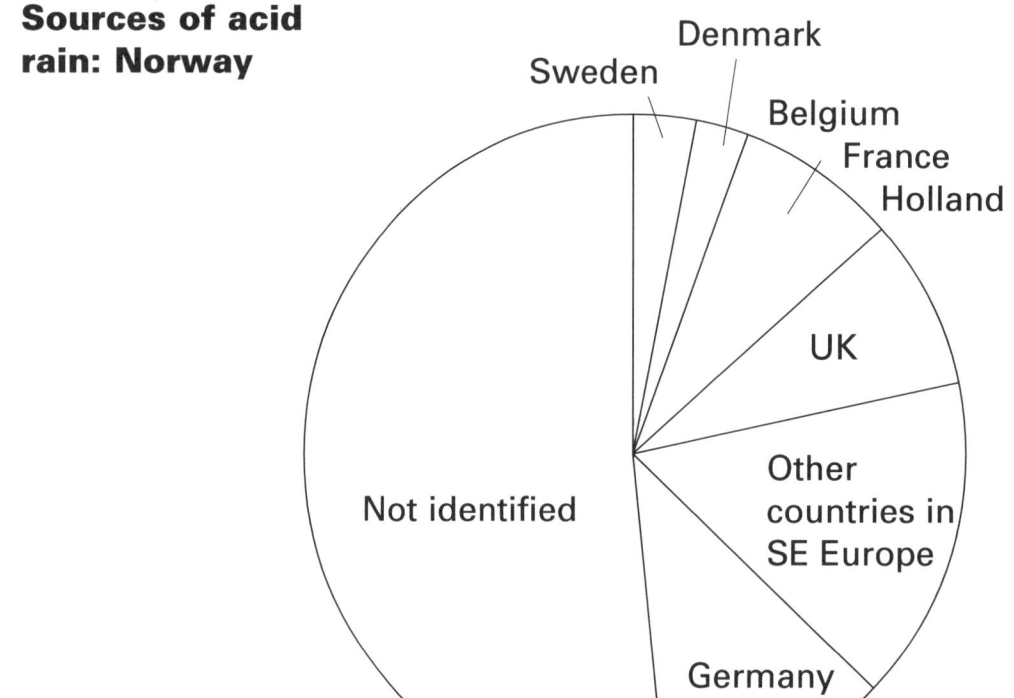

Sweden
Denmark
Belgium
France
Holland
UK
Other countries in SE Europe
Germany
Not identified

Pollution statistics

● The Global Environment Monitoring System calculated that more than 600 million people living in cities were exposed to levels of sulphur dioxide above the recommended limit.

● Over one billion people breathe air containing amounts of particles such as dust, soot and hydrocarbons well above the World Health Organisation maximum.

● In parts of Eastern Europe (in particular the Czech and Slovak Republics, Hungary and Poland), air pollution is particularly high. It is estimated that in Russia 50 million people are exposed to air pollution at a level ten times the recommended limit.

● Cities like Madrid, Paris and Milan also suffer pollution problems with acceptable limits exceeded.

● China also has high levels of pollution, the city of Beuxi was once described as the most polluted city in the world.

● In some parts of South America, such as Brazil and Mexico, pollution is a constant problem. One city had only 54 days in a whole year when the purity of the air limits were acceptable – some schools had to be closed for a whole month.

● Lakes in southern Norway and Sweden have been so affected by pollution from acid rain that there are no fish left in them. 50% of German forests are affected by pollution from acid rain.

PHOTOCOPIABLE

BUILDING HEALTHY ENVIRONMENTS: Pollution – who's to blame?
Pollution – a worldwide problem? Page 62

Actions to improve air pollution – are they enough?

● Many countries have set targets to reduce sulphur dioxide emissions by at least 30%.

● Emissions of oxides of nitrogen are also to be reduced by at least 30%.

● All cars sold in Europe must have catalytic converters – reducing sulphur dioxide emissions.

● Emissions of sulphur dioxide from power stations across Europe and America have been reduced.

● Japan has set strict controls on sulphur emissions from car exhausts but the increase in the number of cars over the last ten years has brought the problem back.

Other schemes to reduce pollution include:

● Cutting the number of car journeys to work by requiring employees to share cars or work more from home.

● Placing restrictions on even minor polluters such as lawnmowers and barbecues.

Role cards

Parents You are divided in your opinions about the closure. Half of you want the school to stay open – it's a good school and it's convenient. The other half thinks that a move to a new, bigger school would be better for the children.	**Local shopkeepers** You are opposed to the closure of the school. The children and parents support your shops and you would lose money if they went to school elsewhere.
Teachers You are opposed to the closure of the school. You think that it is a good school and has successful results. You don't want to move to another school and some of you are afraid that you might lose your jobs.	**Local property developers** You believe that the site could be used to build a few luxury houses which would sell very easily because of the position. You also think that this building work would create jobs and be good for the community.
Governors You are opposed to the closure of the school. It achieves good results, serves the needs of the local community and has a very pleasant group of teachers and children.	**Children** You do not want to change school. You like the school and you are afraid you will be split up from your friends.
Local councillors As councillors representing the whole community you have to argue for closing the school on the grounds that it is not large enough and numbers will continue to fall over the next five years. The children would be better off moving to a new, bigger school.	**Education Authority representatives** You have to defend your decision to close the school. It's small, and will get smaller over the next few years. There is a bigger and better-equipped school for the children to move to.

PHOTOCOPIABLE

BUILDING HEALTHY COMMUNITIES: Who cares for...?
Who cares for... places? Page 68

Project cards

✁

Cleaning up a stretch of the local canal **£100 000**	Providing a covered bus shelter with seats in the village square **£25 000**
Providing more facilities and cleaning up the local park **£80 000**	Building a play area for young children **£120 000**
Planting more trees and flowers in the centre of the village square **£30 000**	Extending the community hall and putting in new equipment **£130 000**
Putting seats and benches and creating a picnic area on the outskirts of the village **£40 000**	Opening a new swimming pool **£200 000**
Providing improved toilets in the village **£35 000**	Improving the local field for football and cricket pitches **£80 000**

Education cards	
To teach Spanish or German in school	To ban football in the school playground
To abandon Sports Day	To refurbish the school library
To extend the school day until 5pm	To provide three computers in each classroom
To attend school only on four days	To stop providing school dinners

PHOTOCOPIABLE

BUILDING HEALTHY COMMUNITIES: Who decides about...?
Who decides about... our work? Page 80

Name _____   Date _____

Wanted

TELEVISION NEWSREADER
(Children's Television)

The Broadcasting Company for Great Britain (BCGB) wish to appoint a newsreader for the children's news programme. This is an exciting new addition to children's television.

The successful applicant should know something about:

The successful applicant should be able to:

We are looking for the sort of person who is:

SPORTS MONTHLY

Top athletes warn that more money is needed to keep Great Britain competitive

Some of the best British athletes yesterday warned the Government that more money was needed if Great Britain was going to continue competing at world-class level.

"We are still not getting the level of financial support that other European countries give their athletes", said one top sprinter, "and we need to be spending our time training. We cannot afford the time to be searching for sponsorship."

These comments came only days after publication of a report that criticised the amount of time allocated to athletics in schools.

A spokesperson for the committee responsible for the report said that very little money was available for athletics in schools and so it often became the 'poor relation' of football, rugby and cricket.

PHOTOCOPIABLE

BUILDING HEALTHY COMMUNITIES: Who decides about...?
Who decides about... our leisure? Page 81

Name _____ Date _____

Leisure proposal

We propose to develop a:

There is a need for this development because:

The suggested location for this development is:

The facilities it would offer would include:

The people who would use it would be:

Customers would be attracted by:

BRACKTON GAZETTE

Police condemn young hooligans!

A spokesperson for the local police force yesterday launched a scathing attack on some of the young people of the area. She described them as 'mindless hooligans with no thought for the harm and distress their stupid behaviour causes'.

She went on to quote recent incidents in which local youths were involved, including shoplifting, damage to cars, theft of garden furniture, graffiti and threatening behaviour to old people. She listed numerous other activities which were described as 'the actions of irresponsible idiots'.

The police are planning to crack down very hard on young people caught behaving in this way and it is possible that parents may also be targeted.

PHOTOCOPIABLE

BUILDING A HEALTHY FUTURE: **A just and fair society**
How do we define wealth and poverty? Page 87

Name _____   Date _____

What is wealth?

This is a picture of the Owens family – their neighbours regard them as a 'wealthy' family. Draw on this sheet evidence that you think would prove that this description of them is true.

BUILDING A HEALTHY FUTURE: *A just and fair society*

How do we define wealth and poverty? Page 87

The poverty trap

Here are some recent statistics and government statements about poverty.

- The average income for a family with three children in Britain is £220 a week. Poverty is defined as living on less than half that figure.

- 12 million people in this country live in relative poverty (25% of the population). This is three times as many as in 1979.

- The UK is ranked 14th behind countries such as Germany, Japan and Australia, in the United Nations Development Programme's poverty index.

- One-fifth of UK adults are illiterate.

- The gap between the rich and the poor continues to widen all across the world – 20% of the world's population consumes 86% of goods and services.

- 4 million children in the UK live in poverty. This is three times more than in 1975.

PHOTOCOPIABLE

BUILDING A HEALTHY FUTURE: **A just and fair society**
Why do people work? Page 88

Is this work?

Discuss whether you think the people in these pictures are working.
Give your reasons.

A fair world?

How evenly are the world's resources distributed?

The gap between the rich and poor people in the world is growing. In general terms it is a division between the rich, developed countries of the north and the poor, developing countries of the south. Only one-fifth of the world's population lives in the rich developed countries, yet they consume two-thirds of the world's resources. This unequal distribution concerns many people.

	Developing country	Developed country
Number of children in a family	🚶🚶🚶🚶	🚶
Energy used (cooking, heating, travel, making goods)	🛢	🛢🛢🛢🛢🛢🛢🛢🛢🛢🛢 🛢🛢🛢🛢🛢🛢🛢🛢🛢🛢 🛢🛢🛢🛢🛢🛢🛢🛢🛢🛢 🛢🛢🛢🛢🛢🛢🛢🛢🛢🛢
Amount of money available per person if shared out	💵	💵💵💵💵💵💵 💵💵💵💵💵💵 💵💵💵💵💵
How much energy in daily food eaten by each person	🌾🌾🌾🌾	🌾🌾🌾🌾🌾🌾 🌾

Key: 🚶 Children   🛢 One barrel of oil   💵 1000 dollars   🌾 2000 kJ

This diagram shows the differences in the amount of resources which a person in each of the two countries uses and the typical daily calorie intake per person per day.

PHOTOCOPIABLE

BUILDING A HEALTHY FUTURE: A just and fair society
How we define the terms 'healthy' and 'unhealthy?' Page 90

Resources available to a ten year old in Cameroon

This information compares the resources available to children from rich and poor families.

POOR	RICH
Food Starchy food due to their limited means (cassava, maize, yam, potatoes and rice). They may have three meals of the same food nutrients each day – their unbalanced diet causes poor growth.	A healthy mixture of fats, carbohydrates, iron and proteins. Three square meals a day, taken along with snacks. This variety leads to health and growth.
Housing Houses are built of plant material, mud blocks, mat and thatches. There is no distinction between the kitchen and the living room. They are not well-protected from the elements. Houses are often too small and overcrowded with large families. They are badly ventilated and often promote ill health.	Houses are large, well furnished and comfortable. They are well ventilated, tiled, air-conditioned and have water heaters available.
Water supply Water comes from standing/running steams, wells and rain water. Some of it is quite clean but it is untreated so germs and fungi are present. The amount available depends on the weather – it is scarce in the dry season. Pipe-borne water is rare; if present at all, it is shared by many people. There will be one tap to cater for about 300 people, financed by the local council.	Pipe-borne water is available in their homes. It is clean and treated by the government, though with negligence at times.
Clothing Limited clothing according to their means. Little choice of colour. About 5000 Cameroon francs is spent by each person in one year.	Rich people have plenty of clothing and have access to a wide variety of styles. They spend approximately 200 000 Cameroon francs per person, per year.

BUILDING A HEALTHY FUTURE: A just and fair society
How we define the terms 'healthy' and 'unhealthy'? Page 90
PHOTOCOPIABLE

POOR	RICH
Health There are no clinics and people rely heavily on traditional doctors. There are only a few, traditional doctors. (Patient/doctor ratio is 1:800). There are no hospitals only health posts. Access to help is difficult – midwives or health posts are often far off.	Clinics are limited and expensive, but they go there instead of hospitals where good services can't be guaranteed. There are only three to six doctors in each hospital depending on the town. There will be only one hospital per town and a few private clinics. Access to help is often difficult.
Transport This varies depending on the need. They travel more when they have health needs and during Christmas holidays when their parents have raised some money from the sale of their produce. Travel is by horse, camel or car. Most people walk long distances.	Not restricted – by all modern methods – car, plane, train and so on.
School Class size depends on the number of schools in the area (60–120). Resources are very limited (chalk, blackboard and the immediate environment). Students lack even the basic materials.	Classes are relatively small, between 45–50 pupils. They have unlimited resources, including computers and televisions.
Entertainment Storytelling and traditional games such as cards or hide and seek.	Television, music, games, radio and picnics.
Toys The poor depend on home-made toys. Children make toy vehicles out of stocks and bamboos. Parents may buy them one toy for special occasion – 2000 Cameroon francs.	The rich have all kinds of toys made in factories. Some families may spend 150 000–200 000 Cameroon francs a year for toys only.
Holidays Both the rich and the poor have their normal school holidays. Going out of the local environment would depend on the socio-economic status of the parents. While the poor stay at home to work with their parents on the farm, the rich visit family friends and relatives in and out of the country.	

Resources available to a ten year old in Germany

Food
Breakfast: bread rolls with jam, cheese or cold meat and hot chocolate drink.
Lunch: main meal – warm main course, usually with meat, vegetables and
salad, potatoes, or noodles and some sort of sweet – ice-cream, jelly or fruit.
Evening: bread, cold meats, cheese.

Housing
A typical family owns a three- or four- bedroom house. Each child has his or
her own room.

Water supply
Unlimited drinking water is available from a mains supply. The quality of this
is tested regularly by the Health Office.

Clothing
A typical child will possess a large amount of shoes and clothing for all
seasons and sporting activities. Up to 3000 Deutchmark will be spent on each
child each year.

Health
Medical help is freely available. People in Germany usually have medical
insurance and free choice of doctor. No waiting list for normal operations.

Transport
Transport to school is usually by bicycle and families will have cars. There is
easy access to other methods of transport.

School
Average class size 25 pupils. Usually well-equipped with IT resources.

Entertainment
Nearly every household has colour TV with 20 channels, as well as a video
recorder and stereo system.

Toys
A typical child would have a large number of expensive toys.

Holidays
At least four weeks per year with the main family holiday usually camping in
some European country, such as Greece or Spain.

BUILDING A HEALTHY FUTURE: A just and fair society

Why do people break the laws of our society? Page 91

TORRINGTON GAZETTE

MAYOR EXPRESSES CONCERN AT INCREASE IN TEENAGE CRIME

Torrington's mayor said that he was bitterly disappointed with the latest crime figures among teenagers.

'I can't understand it,' said the mayor. 'Why do they feel it necessary to damage cars, break into people's property, drop litter and plaster the place with graffiti? They don't seem to have any pride in their town anymore.'

One group of teenagers interviewed by our reporter said that they had nothing to do in the town and that they couldn't afford to pay for any leisure activities. They claimed that all they could find to do was ' just fool around'. They also claimed that all the stories were greatly exaggerated.

One resident, whose garden was vandalised, has threatened to take the law into his own hands. 'If they come anywhere near my property again, they can look out! They'll get more than they bargained for next time – I'm not going to stand idly by and let them rampage through my garden leaving a trail of damage without putting up a fight!'

Name _____   Date _____

Working women

Look at these pictures and discuss, with your partner, the types of jobs that you would expect to find women doing in these locations.
Write the words down as they come to your mind.

BUILDING A HEALTHY FUTURE: A just and fair society
What is equality of opportunity? Page 92
PHOTOCOPIABLE

Equal opportunities!

Statistics, though very important, can sometimes be rather boring!
Turn some of these facts and opinions into an attractive leaflet or brochure.

1 In December 1999:

Men's full-time employment was up 62 000

Women's full-time employment was down 2 000

Men's part-time employment decreased by 16 000

Women's part-time employment increased by 29 000

The number of unemployed men was down by 12 000

The number of unemployed women was up by 8 000

2 Average hourly earnings for men working full-time – £9.57

Average hourly earnings for women working full-time – £7.79

The gender pay gap was the narrowest ever with women (in full-time work) earning 80.9% of men's earnings

3 In 1999 over 7 500 people sought help from the Equal Opportunities Advice Services Section. A further 16 000 people asked for general advice.

This dispels 'the myth that women have achieved equality'.

4 71% of young women (compared to 25% of men) said that an employer's commitment to equal pay would influence their job choice.

98% of women believe that they should be paid the same as men for doing the same job.

5 67% of IT and 96% of engineering places on apprenticeship schemes are taken up by males (average wages £140 and £115).

80% of places in business administration and 92% in hairdressing are taken up by females (average wage £107 and £62).

PHOTOCOPIABLE

BUILDING A HEALTHY FUTURE: **What sort of future?**
What sort of… technology? Page 96

Name _____   Date _____

Advances in technology

Discuss the technological advancements illustrated in these pictures.
Rate them (on a scale of 1–10, where 1 is low, and 10 is high) to indicate
their impact on our society.

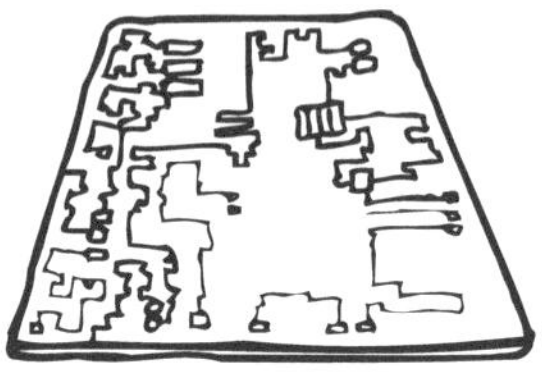

Classrooms

Name _____   Date _____

Personal profile

First draw a picture in the space below that represents 'you'. Then cut out the pieces below for your personal profile choosing the ones that you think best describe how you are developing as a person. Finally stick the pieces around your picture.

✂

Working well with others	Leadership	Accepting other people's opinions
Patience	Dealing with people's problems	Taking responsibility
Self-discipline	Reliability	Listening to what other people say
Honesty	Making good decisions	Willing to compromise
Self-confidence	Sharing ideas	Coping well with disagreements